JESUS CHRIST THE SAME

JESUS CHRIST THE SAME

THE SHAFFER LECTURES FOR 1940 IN
THE DIVINITY SCHOOL OF YALE UNIVERSITY

JAMES MOFFATT

Hon. D.D. (St. Andrews, Oxford), D.Litt.

ABINGDON–COKESBURY PRESS

New York   *Nashville*

JESUS CHRIST THE SAME
Copyright, MCMXL
By Whitmore & Stone

SET UP, ELECTROTYPED, PRINTED AND BOUND BY THE CLERMONT PRESS AT DOBBS FERRY, NEW YORK, UNITED STATES OF AMERICA

To

THOSE AMONG THE WISE AND THE
UNLEARNED WHO KNOW BETTER
THAN THE WRITER WHAT HE HAS
DONE HIS BEST TO DELINEATE IN
THE SIGNIFICANCE OF THEIR LORD
AND HIS.

CONTENTS

A HUNDRED YEARS AGO THERE WAS A HISTORICAL PAINTER in London who had one artistic ambition. He desired to draw the face of Jesus Christ. Four times he tried, first in a picture of the entry into Jerusalem, on which he labored for six years; it was eventually bought and brought over to the United States. Then he painted the raising of Lazarus, as well as the agony in Gethsemane, and an unfinished sketch of the crucifixion. Benjamin Haydon had a touch of genius in his art. He was honored by some of the brightest spirits in his day, from Wordsworth to Sir Walter Scott. Indeed his friend Keats proudly declared that there were three things at which one might rejoice in contemporary England: Wordsworth's "Excursion," Hazlitt's depth of critical taste, and Haydon's pictures. As it happened, none of these four religious pictures satisfied either the artist or his public. Probably no drawing of Christ ever has or ever will. Some of us indeed may have come to desire nothing more than the face of the wonderful child, not a baby but a little boy, in the arms of the Sistine Madonna; it is the divine face of a perfectly natural child, but we are haunted by the slight suggestion of trouble in eyes that seem to foresee mysterious pain and agony to come, even as he faces us with a re-assuring look of quiet mastery and grave confidence. What Raphael's genius did with the face of the young Jesus, Haydon failed to do with the full-grown Christ, however. The results of his work in the studio fell short of his dream. Yet his method was admirable, and that is the main point for us. There was a genuinely religious vein in Haydon's queer character. He once wrote in his autobiography, "The moment I touch a great canvas, I think I see my Creator smiling on all my efforts; the moment I do mean things for mere subsistence, I feel as if he had turned his back, and what's more I believe it." In 1817, as he was beginning to plan his picture on the entry into Jerusalem, he jotted down this sentence: "I resolved to acquire the fundamental principles of perspective, of which I did not know enough. I earnestly prayed that I might conceive and execute such a picture of the head of Christ as would impress the Christian world." While the artist sought reverently to paint a picture of his Lord, he was well aware that he must master the technique of his art in order to achieve his end. Haydon prayed as he painted, but he did not fail to attend to the prosaic details of a matter like perspective as he set to work on the huge canvas, realizing that the one without the other would be of no avail.

The aim of this essay is to consider some of the relevant evidence for the divine humanity of our Lord in historical perspective. This does not mean that the historical method of approach is one thing, and the

10

devotional another, as though mental integrity and moral affinity could only thrive apart in the quest for a real Jesus. Such a notion belongs to prejudices of the street and the study which are no longer tenable. Here as elsewhere it might be said that the inquirer uses a binocular glass, and it is of primary importance to see that the lenses correspond. Otherwise the vision is out of focus. But, granted that the method is not one-sided, it is not unreasonable to believe that an inclusive effort to identify Jesus Christ may lead to the conclusion that the intuition of the Church is borne out by the perspective of historical research into primitive traditions. The thesis of the following pages is by no means new. It is a case of *non nova sed nove* over again. The attempt is to indicate afresh, in the light of our newer knowledge, how nothing is more probable than that he who lived on earth for a few years was the same Christ whom his followers worshipped as Lord, that no new Jesus was created by any syncretistic movement in the first Christian century, that there is a unity in the unsolved mystery of his person which is not only real but the real cause underlying the various interpretations of his life and work, and that later experiences of the Church repeatedly imply a continuity of communion with him which is deeper than any inner or outer change of the faith. In other words, by criticizing criticism as well as tradition, we are on the way to a definite, constructive conviction that in a deep sense Jesus Christ is the same for us as he has ever

11

been for our predecessors, little as we may be able to use some of their precise language about him, and also that there is no other Jesus visible or possible on the horizon of a faith which can be seriously called Christian.   But in order to recognize how the data converge upon this conclusion, it is imperative that the study of historical perspective be taken honestly and thoroughly.

i

One writer in the New Testament urges his readers to defend or contend earnestly for "the faith once for all delivered to the saints."   It is not always easy to understand the dislike of some moderns for this phrase. There is nothing reactionary or stereotyped about it in its context.   For Christianity does start with some definite convictions, which make it what it is; they are dynamical convictions about the significance of Jesus Christ to God and man, not for faith simply but for the faith of those who, as the writer adds, worship "the only God, our Saviour through Jesus Christ our Lord." This faith was not a commonplace of religion, nor a fine opinion casually dropped into the world.   It was God's truth, once for all rooted in the belief of the Church, belonging to the rank and file of those who are inside the community of God.   It was a vital possession, to be preserved at all costs, a magnificent heritage on which to live; and the basis was Jesus Christ in an incomparable position.   So the good Judas argued,

12

appealing to the apostolic confession of faith, which was not a formula; like all the primitive confessions it was sung or recited.

One must admit that this phrase about "the faith once for all delivered to the saints" has too often been made an excuse in some communions for taking no trouble to think about the faith, as if unquestioning acceptance of formulas were the true defense of Christianity. But it was not so in the early Church. For various reasons a phrase used about Jesus, or even a phrase used by Jesus, was re-interpreted or replaced. One expression after another was employed to set forth his significance. At the present day phrases like the Son of man, the Word, or the Son of God, ought to puzzle some of us more than they do; if we are not puzzled by them, it is probably because we are interpreting them in a more or less conventional and inadequate fashion, reading into them modern notions of our own instead of exercising our minds to understand their historical import for the foundation of the faith. Indeed people have frequently sheltered behind this phrase of St. Judas, not only to avoid asking questions about their faith in the Lord but in order to discourage others from raising inconvenient queries which seem to unsettle an ancient creed or a modern rite. Praying people are the strength of any church. But they have now and then weakened the appeal of their religion as they endeavored, not without success, to hinder progressive spirits from seeking and finding new light on the ancient truth of the faith. Some praying folk would do better to pray less and think more; it would be well for them and for their fellows if they would open their minds to receive fresh messages from God as well as open their lips in order to speak to him. For if to labor is to pray, as we are sometimes reminded, to think may be also a form of prayer, since genuine prayer is laying one's life open to the Spirit of the living God for direction. While the fuller knowledge of what Jesus Christ is and means to us may be said to rest upon certain primary convictions which have been held intuitively from the very dawn of the faith and transmitted by generation after generation of real saints, this has involved, and it still involves, the use of all our faculties in response to any newer knowledge of the truth as it is in Jesus.

St. Judas issued his pamphlet or manifesto against some who were so spiritual that they condoned loose living as being merely ethical. He knew that their perverse spiritual interpretation of Christianity, with a conception of God as redeemer but not as creator and of Christ as only semi-divine, led to conduct that denied and disowned the Lord. Even in this form, the error is a recurring danger in some circles of the Church. But the point is that the writer was concerned about religious people who held a sub-Christian idea of Jesus. The fear of this ought to rouse the faithful in every age to ask themselves if their faith in the Lord Jesus is intellectually and morally adequate, and to be on their guard against any interpretation, however specious, which means a practical denial of him in ordinary life. Round the central significance of Jesus in the faith some draw humanistic outlines which, like most outlines of history, are out of line with the relevant data of the problem. But this tendency is provoked by, as in turn it provokes, a nervous disinclination to discuss or at any rate to re-open the question. Today more than ever it is urgent to investigate the new dimensions given long ago to faith and history alike by the revelation of Jesus Christ as Lord of men and Son of God, the more so since this has never been held unthinkingly without damage to vital Christianity. One has only to look over the collection of writings in the New Testament to find evidence for the extraordinary impetus given to thought by this revelation. The very need of bringing out the differences between this faith of the churches and the Jewish or pagan beliefs of its environment, led, through some painful differences of opinion, to a penetrating consciousness of what was involved in the confession of Jesus as Lord. Had Christians in that age been full of what George Eliot called "the right of the individual to general haziness," there would have been no great literature produced. For great literature implies a vital impulse of life and hope, and in the writings which were afterward collected into the New Testament canon such an impulse was derived from the writers' vision of God in the Lord Jesus Christ. That is "the faith once for all delivered to the saints." If it is ever surrendered to any new theory of a God who is too spiritual to be the God of creation or of a Christ who was a deified man, all hope for vital Christianity is lost. To hold it against such attacks is for Christians to "build themselves up" on the faith of the apostles' revelation, and that, for every thoughtful primitive Christian, implied mental as well as moral energy within the fellowship.

ii

It is possible that some traditions of Jesus existed in non-Christian sources, but no reliable trace of these has yet emerged. Practically all we know about Jesus is derived from twenty-seven small books which were written within half a century after the apostle Paul dictated his first letter. They came to be gathered into the New Testament collection as we now have it. In dealing with them we are studying an age when there was no New Testament, not even the idea of a New Testament. The Bible of the Church was its Greek Old Testament. There the Church found anticipations and predictions of their Lord; but these twenty-seven more or less artless writings among others were spontaneous, occasional productions of the Christian mission in small communities round the Mediterranean basin, worshipping God and the Lord Jesus Christ. The groups had a simple organization, which varied. They had no written creed, any more than Judaism

16

had. Their Gospels and Epistles differ in size and shape and outlook. They reveal differences of level and varying depths of belief. Some are anonymous. But the one name common to all of them is the name of Jesus. Most were written independently of the others, though Mark's Gospel was used by Matthew and Luke, and the influence of the apostle Paul's original mind may possibly be traced here and there outside his own letters. But each writes about Jesus for himself, and writes of him as supreme.

There is no reason to suppose that any important stories or sayings of Jesus may have been lost in the disappearance of those early Gospels which failed to win entrance into the canon, and which are mainly or merely known to us in fragments cited by early writers of the second and third centuries. It is not likely that, even if any complete copies turned up among newly found papyri, they would yield serious evidence for modifying the tradition of the canonical Gospels. Thus we possess enough of the so-called Gospel of Peter to make us agree with the decision of bishop Serapion who discouraged its use. And its use was limited and very local. Upon the whole the extra-canonical items which have been preserved are secondary and derivative. How and where and why the four Gospels came to be selected for their supreme position remains a mystery. But it is a clear case of the survival of the fittest. For all practical purposes we possess in them sufficient material to estimate the scope and limits of

17

the tradition about Jesus which was required to answer the purposes of the living Church. Any Gospel fragments that have turned up among the papyri are on the fringe of the original tradition. What they furnish is sometimes of literary and even of historical interest, but not of primary historical importance.

iii

One aid to a correct perspective is a minute study of these classical documents in the light of contemporary life and thought. This is far from being futile or merely a matter of antiquarian interest. It is a discipline which trains the eye to see the reality of Jesus, and at the same time it prevents us from reading into the record more or less sub-Christian notions of a later period. The latter is a real danger in some quarters. Not all the experiences of Christian people are Christian, but they sometimes like to find a sanction for these in the New Testament. Or, in default of that, they justify them as legitimate developments of the faith. If it is urged that the New Testament ignores such beliefs or practices, they sometimes ignore the New Testament, as the Roman Catholic lady admitted to her priest.[1] She had been telling him how highly she valued the visions of Saint Gertrude and Blessed Margaret Mary, a thirteenth-century German mystic belonging to the Benedictine order and a French visionary of the seventeenth century. "They tell us

[1] Tyrrell, *Lex Credendi*, pp. 24, 25.

18

about our Lord, and without them one would know nothing of him." Naturally the priest asked, "Do you ever read the Gospels?" "Oh, no, they are so dry!" It is no less erroneous to take the New Testament as a mere dossier of immature documents which reflect a distant, rather dull and dry stage of Christianity, than it is to regard Gospels and Epistles as a sort of lawbook for the Church. The latter ends in biblicism. The former fails to understand that the New Testament witnesses not to truths but to the living truth of Jesus Christ, and thus becomes a sort of standard and challenge to tradition.

In other words, while "it is no argument at all against a religious view or moral requirement that it is not taught in Scripture," particularly in the New Testament, "there is a prima facie reason for further consideration of any religious novelty in the fact that it is nowhere suggested in this great and various body of literature, embodying the religious experience which we count as central and normative."[2] That experience has a fundamental quality, for all the different forms which it assumes; it is determined by the life and spirit of Jesus Christ, known not in spite of, but through, the limitations of his earthly life and its record.

A further error of perspective is still more subtle. It besets the critical method itself. Literary pre-occupation with so-called units of tradition easily leads to for-

---

[2] C. C. J. Webb, *Religious Thought in the Oxford Movement*, pp. 25f.

getfulness of the living unity, apart from which the data of the analysis are unintelligible and misleading. The contents of the literature may be so cleverly dissected, or its environment may be so highly colored, that the central figure is thrown out of focus. There are books in which the background and the surroundings are so crowded and decorated that the living Figure in the foreground is almost lost sight of; the Lord becomes practically the effect of certain social and religious tendencies rather than the cause, directly or indirectly, of all that happened. It is for example an absorbing and delicate problem to guess where poetry ends and history begins in several stories, or to gauge the extent to which actual reminiscences are being transmitted in certain strata of the evangelic tradition. But both features at any rate indicate that the Church was conscious of possessing an answer to its difficulties, as it enjoyed the living authority of the Lord who had already spoken and acted as none other did. All four Gospels show radii being drawn to this or that controversial issue on the circumference of local and contemporary interests, but the radii are drawn from a single center. It is an error in perspective when the latter point is treated as secondary or disregarded.

Perspective is not art, but without perspective there is no great art, and without knowledge there is no perspective; it is as important to the truth about Jesus as it is to art, whether the art is architecture or painting. Perspective means the power of seeing things in their

20

right relations and due proportions. It requires train-
ing. Mere interest in the subject is not enough, even
if it be devout. Neither is technical criticism, for criticism is not questioning but judgment, and learning
may abound where judgment is scanty. No subject
connected with history can be treated apart from perspective, and yet, for a variety of reasons, nowhere is
the sense of perspective more easily missed than in
studying the life of Jesus. All religions are historical
in the sense that they have had a history. But Christianity is historical in a deeper and distinctive sense;
it is the religion of a divine revelation made in and
through One whose life on earth entered into the new
manifestation of God's mind and purpose. Our faith
does not consist of some general ideas about God and
man which may be detached from the form in which
they were first announced by a Galilean peasant or
prophet long ago in distant Palestine; it is not a vague
religiosity which employs stories about Jesus as convenient symbols or picturesque material for what
French sociologists call a *représentation,* that is, the
product of a community life which embodies its hallu-
cinations and hopes in the shape of tales about its supposed founder. Historical Christianity itself cannot
be distilled from a historic Jesus. All that we know
of him is through the fellowship and worship of the
Church which looked to him as a Lord whose life had
not ended at death. The New Testament is the literature of a worshipping Church. The Word of God in

21

its pages is a Word of the Cross, of "the" Cross. Hundreds were crucified by the Romans every year in Palestine. It was a common form of execution. But the Church saw one Cross, only one. The perspective of faith in Jesus the crucified lies in recognizing what led up to that Cross and what came out of it, what is still coming out of it. Scientific method refuses to understand effects unless there is a sufficient cause behind them. As Tertullian put it, truth is proved by what it produces.[3] There is indeed much in the story of the Christian faith which cannot be directly assigned to Christianity, but the driving and creative factors that entered into the primitive movement are inexplicable apart from such a personality as the New Testament reflects in Jesus Christ.

Thus it is not possible to represent the birth of Christianity as the idea of universal humanity being released somehow from Jewish nationalism and offered by enthusiastic disciples of Jesus, under the form of a religious symbol, to the disinherited of the ancient world. who were only too glad to welcome it with its progressive apotheosis of a human leader; nor again to explain the primitive gospel as the humanizing of a widespread belief about a divine hero or savior-god from heaven, which happened to take shape in the wistful dreams of some Jews who crystallized it round vague memories of a Galilean prophet, although he had neither claimed to be messiah nor headed any sect or group. The for-

---

[3] *De Anima* ii; testimonium est veritati eventus ipsius.

mer hypothesis, popularized by Loisy, has to assume
that the disciples who started the resurrection faith had
not been in touch with the sharp facts of the crucifixion; as these Galileans knew the tragedy only by
hearsay, their illusion, originated by an enthusiast like
Peter, had no shock to overcome. One day the simple
Peter had a vision; he thought he saw and heard Jesus.
This was all that was required to start the new faith.
The other reconstruction, devised by Guignebert, also
starts with an illusion of Peter; the good man, dream-
ing beside the lake of Galilee, managed to rouse a col-
lective hallucination which luckily became fused with
some of the floating beliefs about hero-gods in the
ethnic world of the day, till a compound was generated
and set in motion. Common to both types of this
guesswork is a belittling of Jesus, and also a cleavage
between later views about Jesus and any eyewitnesses.
The historian at once notices that these two errors of
perspective hang together. "Jesus" and "crucified
under Pontius Pilate" are all that is left of the apostles'
creed, and even "Jesus" is perhaps a cult-name! His
crucifixion was simply another murder, one of the
regrettable miscarriages of justice in history. The so-
called apostles or evangelists who recorded the first
phases of the movement reflect the eager enthusiasm of
the new group, swelled by the accession of heady pagan
converts, not any enthusiasm of Jesus himself. Jesus
is merely needed to give his name to the new form of
syncretism; his function at most is to furnish the casual

occasion for its spontaneous emergence. Naturally eye-witnesses are ruled out. They are as obnoxious to such theorists as to the left wing of Form criticism. The inquirer is informed that there was next to nothing memorable in the Galilean's career; his immediate adherents played no great rôle in the growth of a religion with which neither he nor they had any direct personal connection. Four fifths of the contents of the Gospels are imaginative embodiments of the later community's creed; any memories of what Jesus did or said are based on vague traditions which, as a rule, neither require nor suggest the evidence of eyewitnesses. The Syrian stars looked down, as they still look down, on the grave of an obscure fanatic, whose fame was shaped and whose name was floated into the world by some sudden swirl in a first-century concourse of 'isms and 'ologies, stirring in Palestine or Syria or Asia Minor; but anything known of him at this birth of his religion was second-hand and limited. Belief in a historical miracle like this forms the creed of Loisy and Guignebert.

iv

The weak point of all such estimates was noted by Matthew Arnold in dealing with an earlier form of their common theory. Arnold had the advantage of being a fine literary critic. He had no idea that to study great architecture in literature one should watch stones being dug out of a quarry. The notion that a crucible makes the gold or silver that is poured into it did not appeal to his trained judgment. He had three convictions about the Christianity of the New Testament; that it was of vital moment to his age, that the revelation of Jesus was the essential thing in its record, and that it was our duty to disentangle this from a belief in miracles and dogma which had blurred the apostles' priceless account of "that immense reality, not fully or half grasped by them, the mind of Christ." While the evangelists, he admitted, wrote in perfect good faith, they had been affected by some of "the learned or simple ignorance" of their day. The clue to the mystery lay, for Arnold, not in postulating a creative tendency in group movements or social trends but in the fact that "Jesus, as he appears in the Gospels, is manifestly above the heads of the reporters." This he had to maintain on two fronts, not only against the popular Christianity of the churches but also against men like Strauss and Baur. For by the time that he wrote *God and the Bible,* two years after *Literature and Dogma,* he discovered to his amazement that the Tübingen school had reversed his criterion of criticism. For himself the cardinal guide in reading the Gospels had been, "Jesus over the heads of all his reporters." Now he saw Strauss and Baur assuming and asserting that "in the Fourth Gospel it is the reporter who is above the head of Jesus," and he had no difficulty in seeing that this sort of hypothesis was an inverted pyramid.

We recognize the limitations of Arnold's technique. It is no longer possible for criticism to be satisfied with an effort to detach authentic sayings of Jesus from a somewhat unintelligent expansion of them by the Fourth evangelist. The difference between exposition or interpretation of traditions and a sort of Targumistic reproduction of actual sayings is not so simply solved as that.[4] The traditions in the Fourth Gospel, or indeed in any of the Gospels, are due to the Spirit of God moving on his churches, as they preserved and reported his significance for their own age no less than for those who had met Jesus in Palestine. Yet Arnold's perception was essentially sound. All such interpretations presuppose a Jesus who was no ordinary individual, and to estimate them historically it is necessary to have such an estimate of him as will explain why such astounding authority could be attributed to him. An English traveler in Russia, not long after the revolution, overheard one peasant saying to another, "After all, Jesus lived a long time ago, and he was not so well educated as Lenin and Trotsky." This naïve estimate may still be overheard in some learned books about Jesus; their hypothesis is that the disciples were greater men than the Master, and also that modern knowledge of syncretistic Judaism and primitive community-life in the churches enables us to discover that the Christianity which the disciples wove round their Lord was

---

[4] See the thirteenth chapter of Doctor Streeter's *The Four Gospels;* better still, Dr. Vincent Taylor's paper on "The Johannine Christ-Testimonies" in the *Hibbert Journal* (xxvii, pp. 123-147).

far above anything of which he himself could have been conscious. In repudiating such a notion Arnold was right. To say that Jesus was above the head of his disciples and reporters is a less misleading phrase than any form of the rival assumption that later generations improved upon the limited outlook of a young enthusiast or misguided prophet or pious peasant in Palestine. Such an assumption, in reconstructions offered by men like Bultmann, rests on two notions; one, that Jesus never gave distinct rules to his followers, but that they had to evolve these for themselves in Palestinian communities and Hellenistic circles, the other, that he did not take his followers into his confidence, as the Gospels allege that he did. Neither presupposition is tenable, except on the hypothesis that Jesus is no more to historical research than a vague, mysterious Figure who becomes intelligible only as human relationships are stripped from the record of his appearance on earth. But if there is one thing historically clear in the tradition, it is the care taken by Jesus to train his inner circle of disciples, as a rabbi would do,[5] not only how to preach but to commit his sayings to memory. The very literary form of the latter often points to oral repetition by those whom he had personally taught to remember these deliverances, with a view to their own mission work as catechists and teachers. The primitive oral tradition contained such decisive sayings, in addition to reminiscences of his own dialogues and

---

[5] B. S. Easton, *Christ in the Gospels,* pp. 40, 41.

27

deeds. These may have taken imaginative form, as they were chronicled in view of later situations in the controversies of the later Church, but they are not mere products of imagination. Thus, to cite one instance, the wonderful account of the three temptations of Jesus is a record of inward struggle which forms a masterpiece of description. Look for the artist, however, not in some community-group or in an unknown disciple who depicted the conflict out of his own psychological intuitions, but in Jesus himself; he was the artist to whom we owe the delineation of the profound experience.[6] This critical verdict goes deeper than any other. It suggests a point of view which answers to the data of more items than this in the tradition, by insisting that Jesus himself must somehow have been not only the occasion but the inspiration of similar reminiscences in the record.

Those whose historical conscience has some qualms about positing an insignificant Jesus and a total break between him and his adherents may indeed raise the legitimate question whether it is not possible to unbare a certain amount of tradition about Jesus which has not been overlaid by apostolic interpretation, much as Franciscan scholars sometimes wonder if they cannot get behind Thomas of Celano to more authentic, independent accounts of Francis. But the cases are hardly parallel. There is no hope in trying to recover some imaginary pure version of Christianity prior to the

---

[6] So M. Albertz in *Die Synoptischen Streitgespräche*, pp. 47, 48.

time when, a year or two after the crucifixion, the mission to non-Jews started with such unexpected consequences for the development of the faith in spheres of thought and of action. The Gospels, all written after that epoch-making experience, reflect, upon a fair analysis, not mainly, and certainly not merely, the results of the advance but also the cause which produced such a transformation of outlook. Call the outcome Pauline or Hellenistic. But the apostle's dominant concern was in Christ as a living Saviour for man, Jew or Gentile. The Fourth evangelist might go to religious philosophy for the category of the Word, but he saw and sought to make others see Jesus coming into the world as "the real light that enlightens every man." These and the other New Testament writers were not conscious of any new gospel; they derived all these changes of outlook from the same Jesus, known in the living tradition of the communities, which still throbbed under the weighty, direct impact of his revelation. "There is no salvation by anyone else, nor even a second Name under heaven appointed for us men and salvation," none but Jesus.

v

This line of interpretation is confirmed by the fact that eyewitnesses of Jesus had been from the first testifying to him, as through their words and otherwise the impetus of the Spirit moved the churches in their fellowship and worship. What is authentic in the his-

tory of any individual rests upon the report of eyewitnesses. Someone saw, someone heard, what had happened. Someone else probably reported it, before it
finally reached literary form. This is a commonplace
of history which the learned analyst or romancer often
appears to forget in studying the records of Jesus.
Undoubtedly there are more than matter-of-fact statements in their pages. One need not rush to the conclusion that, when a story about Jesus was told in the
primitive Church,

> All who told it added something new,
> And all who heard it made enlargement too.

But tales about him, as well as the tales or parables he
told, were not passed on without adaptation and altera-
tion; many of the miracle or wonder stories baffle us to
know what core of fact is at the heart of them, if any.
Still, the nucleus of most tales is beyond question authentic. As for the sayings, while no one would dream
of attempting to identify Christianity with explicit
sayings of Jesus, it is right to say that historically we
have as much reason to believe as to doubt that early
Christians on the whole were as scrupulous as the
apostle Paul[7] in distinguishing an authentic command
of the Lord, transmitted by his first hearers, and a regu-
lation of the later Church which sought to obey his
Spirit and to express what they believed to be his mind
upon problems of their own day and generation.

---

[7] 1 Cor. vii. 10, 25.

30

But sayings and stories cannot be sharply divided. The same principle applies to both, viz. that nothing can be more unreal than to imagine that they were preserved simply because they were thought to be of use to later groups of Christians within and outside Palestine. When it is remembered, as literary theorists sometimes fail to do, that Jesus went about doing good for two or three years, mixing with thousands of his fellow-countrymen, tales of what so remarkable a man did and said were bound to be told about him after his death, especially by those who now shared the resurrection faith. The resurrection made people sometimes see more in them than they had done at first. But stories such as the tradition preserves are in the main perfectly natural reminiscences; they tell exactly the kind of thing that is caught up by memory of a wonderful healer and teacher, both in his more homely moments and in loftier hours.

The last-named point is specially important. It is essential to a true perspective that we recognize enough evidence within the Gospels to show how Jesus was himself conscious of being more than a prophet or a teacher, and how he knew himself to be Son of God as no ordinary person did. Those nearest to him regarded him as One who had often an air of awe and mystery, of tension and of trenchant authority, as though he lived in two worlds. This is implicit in Mark's outline; the Fourth Gospel itself frequently does no more than elaborate some such primitive features. To de-

31

fine or to describe the meaning of the relevant data may not be easy or even possible. The Gospels are not studies in the self-consciousness of the Lord. Yet for all their discrepancies and divergences, for all their traces of later reflection and heightening reverence playing on the stories of his earthly life and producing prose-poems like those at the start and the close of Matthew and Luke, the gospel tradition does presuppose some such self-consciousness. To his followers from the outset, before, no less than after, the resurrection, he was as one who seemed to be sensible of a unique vocation, in which he was destined to reveal God to men and men to themselves by his inauguration of the divine reign or realm on earth. This is not to be dismissed as a purely posthumous halo. While Jewish conceptions and Hellenistic influences have contributed to various phases of primitive thinking about the gospel, no mere synthesis of these could have produced such an estimate of Jesus Christ as is required in order to account for the honor and dignity with which he is spontaneously invested in Gospels and Epistles alike. These human documents are unintelligible apart from a nucleus of first-hand evidence for a divine core and center in the figure which they serve to represent, evidence that goes back to his immediate disciples. An adequate historical inquiry does not leave the intercourse between the Master and his followers in a luminous haze. It points to the conviction that the exodus of Christianity during the first century of its existence from rabbinic Judaism into a larger world where it was neither absorbed nor recast into something rich and strange, implies a genesis of its essential characteristics which must be prior to the resurrection, and without which neither the resurrection nor the resurrection faith is really conceivable. The proper focus for understanding his life lies here and here only. When the Church, after the resurrection, named his name as they worshipped the one God, this was but the flowering of a seed which he had dropped into the field of faith during his life on earth, to bear fruit of varying excellence, some thirtyfold, some sixtyfold, and some a hundredfold.

vi

From the very start of the Christian movement men were witnessing to the Lord Jesus who had been with him, as they said, "all the time that he went in and out among us, from the baptism of John down to the day when he was taken up from us." Their primary testimony to the resurrection rested on an intimate acquaintance with Jesus during his earthly ministry. When their spokesman, Peter, addressed a group of some sympathetic pagans at Caesarea,[8] they did not require to be told the facts of that ministry; it was familiar to them. Hundreds of eyewitnesses had already talked of it throughout the country. What they welcomed was the interpretation of that mission

---

[8] Acts x. 36-39.

as meant for more than Jews. "You know the message which God sent to the sons of Israel when he preached the gospel of peace by Jesus Christ (he is Lord of all) . . . you know how the word spread over all Judea, how God consecrated Jesus of Nazareth with the holy Spirit and power, and how he went about doing good and curing all who were harassed by the devil; for God was with him. As for what he did in the land of the Jews and in Jerusalem, we can testify to that." The Greek of this passage is puzzling. For one thing, the term rendered "the word" might mean fact no less than story, as the Genevan version tried to persuade English readers; "ye know what thing was done throughout all Jewry." The general sense of the summary is plain, however. This factor of personal testimony entered deeply into the primitive gospel tradition. In attesting the resurrection, it inevitably bore witness in some elementary way to the character and functions of him who had been raised. It is more than a paradox to say that while Jesus "came to preach the gospel, his chief object in coming was that there might be a gospel to preach."[9] Not that this implies any indifference to his teaching and healing ministry on the part of the early Church, as though nothing mattered to them, or ought to matter to us, except the solitary fact that he had died and was believed to have passed through death with a saving act of triumph. Doctor Dale's aphorism simply corresponds to the apostolic tradition of the gospel as

---

[9] R. W. Dale, *The Atonement* (chap. ii).

peace ("God and sinners reconciled"), not as some ethical program of the kingdom in the sense of a reform which had no organic connection with the crucifixion. The full significance of the mission and ministry was first grasped by those who woke to realize what the resurrection meant. Consequently the preaching of the risen Lord in the communities included authentic witness to what had led to the resurrection. If for a time the expectation of his speedy return had more interest for many than actual memories of his life on earth, nevertheless the latter were not allowed to fade.

The range of witness widened into personal testimony borne by those who in visions and other forms of inward experience had a new contact with the risen and reigning Lord. So much so, that "witness borne to Christ" or "the witness of Christ" became one of the synonyms for the gospel. What inspired prophets in the communities, as one of themselves claimed, was the testimony of Jesus.[10] The phrase may mean that the breath or Spirit of all prophecy is either testimony borne by the living Lord or witness borne to him. Probably both were intended, for the prophetic message of witness was a revelation attested by the Lord himself, a revelation of himself which was at once the subject and the impulse of preaching. The evidence of the first three Gospels, for example, indicates that however the term "Son of man" may have been editorially added or used for the simple "man," it repre-

[10] Rev. xix. 10.

sented a self-designation of Jesus, and that this alone explains the subsequent faith and witness of the Church. "With Wellhausen," Reitzenstein admitted,[11] "I can only understand the disciples' faith in the risen One, if during his life he had been already for them no mere man, nay something higher." A title like that of the Son of man on the lips of the historical Jesus affords the psychological and historical nexus between the apostles' testimony and their earlier experience of his personality.

vii

Terms employed by Jesus or applied to him in his mission, conceptions like Messiah, Son of man, the Word, and so forth, must indeed be viewed as more or less organic to his person rather than as logically coherent or mutually exclusive. Such categories were far from being closely defined. All had a variety of associations, some rich and suggestive, but none absolutely normative for the religion of the day, much less for the new belief in Jesus within the churches. They meant at once far less or far more in the case of Jesus than they had as yet done in religious tradition. As categories for him they were not final. They were not even consistent. What determined their new significance was his original relation to God and man. In the early Christian writings we notice how different men employ them in a variety of ways, as they attempt to set forth

---

[11] *Das iranische Erlösungsmysterium*, p. 119.

the sense of what the Lord meant to faith; it is also obvious that he himself used them, that is, terms like Son of man and messiah, in a similarly free fashion.

Thus the authoritative criticisms passed by Jesus upon the religious authorities of his day, as we have them in our texts, have been sometimes shaped or modified by later interests and experiences of the Church in its controversy with Judaism. But, while these variations have to be noted, if we are to reach the authentic attitude of Jesus toward what may be conjectured to have been contemporary religion in Palestine, the tension reflected in such passages goes back to the historical combination of prophetic loyalty and freedom in his own relation to the Law. The forms and content are inexplicable apart from some creative and decisive spirit such as Jesus is reported to have possessed. How this prophetic spirit is connected with his personality, is another question. In all likelihood it was more than prophetic; it was what, for lack of a better term, we may call messianic, and in the Gospels this self-consciousness is explained as one of sonship to God in a special sense. But the point is that, here as elsewhere, the clue to any historical estimate of what the primitive Church believed about him, is to be found in something deeper than its own consciousness of requiring to justify its breakaway from Judaism. Plainly there is what we may call a plus of preaching or edifying motive in the Gospels. The didactic or apologetic or devotional interest is unmistakable. But

37

this only serves to indicate that the story was told and retold because Christianity cannot live on the mere present of its experience, or even on recollections of religious truths enunciated by a supreme prophet. No phase of primitive thought ever declared, "God is one, and Jesus is his prophet." Highly as many valued his prophetic function, they knew how he had believed in himself as no prophet had ever done. The personal note which he struck is an advance on Hebrew tradition, and immensely significant; it witnesses to a consciousness of his vocation which, after the resurrection, was recognized as divine. Whatever Christ was, he was more than a prophet, as Spinoza frankly allowed. It may still be helpful to think of him as a man of God, richly endowed with authority and insight. But "though Christ appears to have announced laws in the name of God, he was not so much a prophet as the mouth of God; God revealed certain truths to mankind by the word of Christ directly."[12] Or, as moderns prefer to put it, the revelation is the revealer, and the revealer lived a human life. "The Word became flesh and dwelt among us." Interpretations of this story presuppose a belief that the life of Jesus was critical and creative, as nothing else was, for the fellowship; in entering into its significance lay all that mattered for the present and the future which he had himself foreseen and over which he had control.

---

[12] *Tractatus Theologico-Politicus* **iv.**

This living core of personal testimony behind the variety of interpretations, is a factor of crucial importance in the genesis of the Gospels. It does not mean that the Gospels are transcripts of first-hand evidence. Reminiscences need not always be accurate. Memory is imaginative as well as retentive. But the fact that from the first there were eyewitnesses who served the Word by their ministry of personal testimony[13] tells against the hypothesis that a story of what Jesus had said or done must be sharply distinguished from a story which suggests what Jesus had meant to the narrator, as though the latter were less credible on that account. A witness to the resurrection, for example, believed honestly that it had occurred, and wished this to be credited by his hearers. The primitive disciples sought to persuade others of what they had themselves not only experienced but tested in the sphere of relevant proof, and ultimately this meant truth in a tale. No other sort of testimony was possible in this case. And on a broader scale, the fact that a witness desired some record of Jesus to be believed does not necessarily discredit the value of his story. It is in the last degree unlikely that the closer men were to the historical Jesus, the more detached they would be. They were not cool reporters of his career but eager to impart what they recollected of it. We get nowhere if we approach the Gospels with a preconceived idea that it is invariably a note of sec-

---

[13] Luke i. 2.

ondary tradition when any stirring or moving touch is to be felt in a narrative. Tradition is indeed apt to become more picturesque as it develops, but that is another matter. The truth is, no theoretical line can be sharply drawn between a testimony of faith and a mere report in this sphere. The nearer we get to the Jesus of history, the less probable it is that any Christian would dream of an impersonal account. It was not in such an objective spirit that he witnessed to his Lord or cared to have anyone else witness. The traditions throbbed in an age of the Spirit which made the faithful glow with rapture and conviction.

By the time these oral tales and traditions took literary form, imagination had begun to play upon them. Yet this does not mean that heightened reverence dazzled the minds of those who compiled the Gospels, until definite memories of Jesus in history became confused or weak. In their sources it is possible to discover sufficient data to render it more than likely that the primitive disciples, in recollecting what had happened to them in the company of Jesus, often saw this wonderful past already beginning to

> "Orb into that perfect star
> We saw not when we moved therein."

Not because their growing awe created out of memory a shining something which had not been previously present in some degree, but because in the light of

40

experience and reflection they now saw some things more clearly that had been always there.

viii

Although the four Gospels, with their resemblances and differences in depicting Jesus, are a unique phenomenon in literature, there are partial parallels in the ancient world. Thus Plutarch's Caesar is not precisely the same as the Caesar of Cicero's letters or the Caesar of Suetonius or again the Caesar of Lucan; yet what they tell of him is more or less in character, despite the fact that their estimates of his career and character vary. In Greece we find a closer and more suggestive parallel to the Gospels, however. There is Socrates. He left no written account of what he said and did. All that we know of him is by hearsay, gleaned from some who were in touch with him, though none of them appears to have had any firsthand knowledge of the master in the earlier period of his life. Plato the philosopher saw more in him than Xenophon the versatile soldier of fortune or Aristophanes the dramatist. Why? Partly because there was more in the mind of Plato than in the other two, more insight, more sympathy with the great sage of Athens, but partly also because, when Plato wrote his dialogues, he was more interested in Socrates than in himself. In one sense and to a real degree, the interests and ideals of both Plato and Xenophon are reflected in their portraits of the master. In both there is evidence of a transfigur-

41

ing process. Yet neither uses Socrates indiscriminately as a mouthpiece for his own opinions. This is particularly true of Plato. Occasionally indeed he is more audible than Socrates, as John is more audible than Jesus in certain sections of the Fourth Gospel. Yet there is a fair case for Platonic scholars who maintain, with full recognition of Plato's original genius, that when he composed the Socratic dialogues he was generally thinking more about Socrates than about himself. These wonderful pieces of literature and propaganda were designed to perpetuate, as it were, the memory of one whose death, it has been said, stopped the moral rot of Greece. Plato's object was to enshrine, if possible, the spirit and character of Socrates in the mind of thoughtful Athenians, so that the next generation might learn from the master to think for themselves. This may sound paradoxical, but it is a serious thesis that in such dialogues we are not to look for a Platonic philosophy, which the author adroitly draped round a tradition of Socrates, but rather for an interpretation by one whose primary aim was to appreciate and expound his revered teacher's wisdom for life. If there is evidence for such a view of Plato's Socratic dialogues, there is at least as good reason to believe that the writers of the Gospels may have been really more interested in transmitting traditions of Jesus, with interpretations of what they had come to see in him, than in shaping casual, scattered recollections into religious philosophies or church

views of their own, which they were supremely anxious
to advocate by constructing more or less imaginary
scenes of the Lord's life on earth.

A cogent example is provided by the call of the first
disciples as told by Mark. "As he passed along the
sea of Galilee, he saw Simon and Simon's brother Andrew netting fish in the sea—for they were fishermen;
so Jesus said to them, Come, follow me and I will make
you become fishers of men. At once they dropped
their nets and went after him." The tale is repeated
by Matthew with one or two stylistic variations. Luke
substitutes for it, at a later stage, another piece of tradition, in which a sudden successful haul by Simon
becomes the means of his accepting the apostolic vocation; the story thus symbolically prefigures the mission
to the Gentiles, and is independently employed in the
last chapter of the Fourth Gospel.[14] But the Marcan
tradition goes back to personal reminiscences of the
actual scene. It is indeed dismissed by some literary
analysts like Bultmann and Dibelius as an unhistorical
legend spun out of a phrase which Jesus may have used
("I will make you fishers of men"), the alleged reasons
being that the Gospels could not have been interested
in psychological relations between Jesus and his followers, and that the summons is too sudden. Neither
argument is in the least convincing. The call may not
be so abrupt as it seems, if there is anything in the

---

[14] E. A. Abbott, *The Fourfold Gospel*, iii, pp. 4-153; Vincent Taylor,
Behind the Third Gospel, pp. 229f.

tradition preserved by the Fourth Gospel that Jesus had already met these men at the revival mission of John the Baptist. But in any case it is an error in perspective, due to learning being allowed to blot out the sense of real life, when critics miss the fact that Jesus must have had amazing powers of attaching men to his personality and mission. There are repeated instances of this, as in the call of Matthew, and the history of religion presents many a parallel. The man of God, the arresting prophet, knows whom to choose and when. It has been noted by a biographer[15] of Francis of Assisi that he possessed this gift. He would, at a moment's notice, summon men to join him naturally and spontaneously. The saint was not copying Jesus; he simply demanded loyalty, as Jesus did, with a look or a quick word, till hearers were won over to the cause at once and forever. One of the least forgettable things in the mind of the first disciples would be the decisive moment that made them disciples. They could not fail to recall the memory of how Jesus first summoned them to his fellowship, and Mark's vivid story enshrines this precisely as it may have happened. It would be retold by the apostles for its own sake as well as to prove their credentials for the mission. At the heart of the primitive tradition many such recollections must have lain, treasured by those who had been eye-witnesses.

It is as artificial to ignore this factor in the genesis

[15] Paul Sabatier, *Vie de S. François d'Assise* (chap. vii).

44

of the Gospels as to suppose either that any tale in which Jesus takes the initiative must be of secondary importance, since he never spoke unless he was questioned or criticized, or again, as some argue, that even the latter sections in the tradition are mainly picturesque reproductions of later controversies which have been dramatically read back into the Palestinian mission of the Lord. This may be true of certain passages in the Fourth Gospel, but it does not apply to the central record of the synoptic tradition. In the first place, one of the results reached by recent criticism,[16] is that the accounts of what is said to have passed between Jesus and his Jewish critics, contain a surprisingly small amount of references to contemporary dissensions and debates in the apostolic Church, a much smaller amount than is popularly assumed to be present in the record. The primary historic value of the latter is upon the whole for what Jesus himself had said in Palestine, rather than for the milieu of gospel writers at Antioch or elsewhere. In the second place, primitive tradition shows Jesus acting upon his followers rather than influenced by them. We find nothing like a sketch of some hero with a group of associates who share his plans and contribute to his achievement. He takes the lead in their intercourse with an autonomy,[17]

---

[16] As in M. Albertz's *Die Synoptischen Streitgespräche*, pp. 59f., 97f., and B. S. Easton's *The Gospel Before the Gospels* (chap. iv, "The Synoptic Perspective").

[17] The present writer has a study of "The Autonomy of Jesus," in *The Expositor* (sixth series), vols. iii-iv.

which reaches its fullest expression in the Fourth Gospel. He does not consult with them. Yet, on the other hand, he does not leave them altogether outside his plan; he imparts his project or secret to the inner group, instead of involving them in a tragedy to which they were entirely strangers. Without a recognition of the historical core in this Marcan tradition, the Easter faith becomes inexplicable. But from this also flows the current of personal testimony throughout the strata of the Gospels. A just perception of these two factors imposes limits upon the hypothesis of the tradition being little more than a freely constructed representation of a life which was but faintly known at firsthand. So far from the figure of Jesus being molded to suit later patterns of the Christian communities, the evidence rather points to the identity of his person. It is no new discovery that, apart from the vivid memories of the Palestinian disciples, the person of Jesus would not be within reach. But a recent corroboration of this is not unwelcome. The verdict comes from a classical scholar,[18] who, approaching the Gospels and gospel-criticism without any theological leanings, finds in the former "a good and trustworthy tradition, from which the few elements that are due to popular imagi-

---

[18] Professor H. J. Rose in two articles on "As It Appears to an Outsider" (*Canadian Journal of Religious Thought*, v, pp. 355-364), and on "Herakles and the Gospels" (*Harvard Theological Review*, xxxi, pp. 113-142), which exhibit the method of a trained expert instead of the amateur speculations which frequently handle the supposed influence of mystery cults and Hellenistic mythology upon the formation of a plastic gospel tradition.

nation can be subtracted with little trouble"; he is impressed by the fact that "when we try to reconstruct their sources, written or oral," we are dealing "with thoroughly honest people, who told a story they entirely believed with no more than a minimum of the distorting medium through which every narrator must see the events which he tries to record." What the Gospels exhibit, in short, is the transmission of singularly credible information about what Jesus was and did, presented often as the answer to questions which had been originally raised or at any rate rendered inevitable by his own mission.

ix

Differences in the portraits go back primarily, though not entirely, to this evidence of the first hearers or eyewitnesses. Contemporaries of a great leader may tell what impressed them in some of his sayings or actions. From their memories come the earliest materials for an interpretation of his career, when that falls to be written. But even eyewitnesses do not always see the same details, or, if they do, they are impressed by different points, owing to temperament or power of perceptiveness. However truthful and interested they may be, it is a well-known fact that surprising variations occur in reports of the same occurrence, even by those who were on the spot. Among bystanders and hearers, some miss what others notice; not all are equally sensitive to the meaning of the incident, or

47

equally quick to seize its significance. In the realization of any historical situation there is what Baron von Hügel called the law of spontaneous variation. The first evidence comes from those who reacted instantly to what they saw and heard; yet, as the event is transmitted through different minds and memories, it does not emerge exactly the same, except in one or two central features. Any efforts to reconstruct what happened are met by the fact that reliable witnesses may be found giving reports which are neither full nor in harmony, and which sometimes seem to be contradictory. But this does not affect the truth that something did happen or that something vital was said at a crucial moment, like the revelation made at Caesarea Philippi, for example, or at the entry into Jerusalem. The variety of testimony does not first appear in later interpretations; it belongs already to the primitive evidence. And it serves to show that a particular event took place at a given time and in a given way. Through vagueness here and confusion there, it is generally possible to arrive at some fairly definite sense of an actual happening, without which these discrepant or partial testimonies would be inexplicable.

The testimonies have indeed reached us along a channel of sympathy and propaganda, but this, it must be repeated, is a characteristic which requires to be fairly judged, if misconceptions are to be avoided. The Gospels are not objective history, written with a dispassionate regard for facts. Their interest in what

48

Jesus had been on earth arose from men who were conscious of his living power and presence in the fellowship and worship of the communities. Their simple records of the Lord were not annals; they were composed by faith for faith, with a purpose in view. But this is no more than we might expect. It no more impairs their validity than the validity of ancient histories in general. Writers of Greek and Latin history had little or no idea of what moderns mean by disinterested interest in history. They had a point of view to defend or to attack. Hardly any, so far as we can judge, dreamed of studying the past for its own sake, whether they were composing memoirs or annals; indeed it is their preferences and prejudices which often make their pages live. Occasionally a historian like Herodotus might be aware of the temptation to patriotic bias. Some took pains to weigh evidence and to sift traditions, discarding current myths, though most paraphrased earlier sources freely without much care for their actual value. The best were particular about the choice of their materials, which for a historian as well as for an architect is as important as any plan of reconstruction; but all had interests, and their interests affected as well as inspired their narratives. Some were perfectly frank in avowing why they wrote at all. Thus Livy's aim was to revive and foster a healthy national spirit, while Polybius held that the study of history contributed to political education. The original motive might be and often was curiosity, or the desire to entertain the reading public of the day; it might be the mere love of storytelling. But authors like Thucydides, Polybius, Josephus, Plutarch, and Diodorus Siculus, or like Livy, Sallust, and Tacitus, confess that their aim is utilitarian. We might fairly call it edifying. Even when they profess to be impartial, their descriptions subtly suggest the particular view which they are advocating. Generally it is to instruct or to improve their contemporaries, to pass a verdict on evildoers, and to uphold ideals of freedom against tyranny; in short, to impress their readers with some political or moral faith. For all their romantic and rhetorical methods, they seek to warn and guide men by compiling narratives of the recent or the remote past, for the benefit of a present generation which was facing a future where similar crises or issues might arise in the life of the State or of civilization. The most objective had an object. There is usually some serious moral in their story, even when it is artistic. The light of a purpose is in the eyes of the recorder, as it was in those who had written the Old Testament histories. Greek and Roman writers depicted things as they were, or as they had been, because they had some idea of how things ought to be. "These things are written," the average historian of old practically says, "that you may be forewarned." Today we read their pages, as we read the Gospels, with an eye to such purposes, endeavoring to allow for tendencies of idealization; we dissect their evidence, probe for their sources of information,

JESUS CHRIST THE SAME

and try to guess how far their prepossessions may have affected their judgment at certain points. We have to note how they invent or accept or adapt legends to serve some purpose, which is more frequently hinted than underlined.

It is an error of perspective, therefore, to isolate the Christian records and to handle them with the tacit presupposition that their contents are upon a lower level of historicity because they were designed to meet a practical end of persuasion. When the primitive Church confessed its faith in God, in the one God, it was far more than faith in the Maker of heaven and earth; it was faith in a transcendent God who made history. To human faith, already in the Old Testament phase, this had been supremely vital. Christians saw the truth of it enlarged and confirmed in the mission of Jesus their Lord. Professor Bury once reminded scholars candidly that to talk about "history for history's sake" was only rational if history could be regarded as a movement of reason. The New Testament witness to Jesus Christ presupposes that in history there is a movement of the divine purpose; the Gospels were written because men had come to believe that in God's revelation through the incarnate Christ they possessed a clue to the mystery and meaning of the world in time. That hypothesis may be set aside; so may the record of it, but not upon the ground that the consciousness of such significance and the desire to transmit it indicate necessarily a symptom of unscientific method or of

51

inferior insight. Why, from Plato to Arrian, everyone who wrote about Socrates did so because he was interested in the personality and teaching of Socrates as an influence likely to be of service to mankind! So far as historical method is concerned, early Christians who wrote the Gospels were doing neither less nor more when they reported the life and sayings of their Lord. Certainly they had a point of view, a rationale or interpretation of the facts. They never meant to be entertaining. Everything and everyone in the Gospels serves as a background to Jesus, though this cannot always be said of modern books about the Gospels. The four evangelists had no idea of meeting the curiosity of outsiders by describing a panorama of Palestinian life in the days of Jesus. It was a commanding view of him as the key to the past, the present, and the future, which determined their selection of the data and the forms into which they cast these data, as they concentrated their attention upon traditions about salient phases in the life which preceded and explained the story of the Passion. In other words, they had a pragmatism of their own. But so, to some extent, had their predecessors and their contemporaries who wrote of episodes or campaigns or dynasties or personalities in another kind of past. Some popular misconceptions about the Gospels would be removed, if it were realized that there is nothing intrinsically inferior or misleading in an approach to history which assumes that writer and readers alike belong to the past under discussion, and that this past not only enters specially and significantly into their present situation but bears upon their future. If this involves partiality, instead of a detached attitude to the story, it is no reflection on their reliability. For judgment in historical matters does not mean impartiality, in the popular sense of the term. It is the duty of a judge to decide for or against a given issue. No doubt, his decision is valuable as it rests on a fair and full study of the relevant evidence. But the final result is a conviction, not a dispassionate opinion. The facts or acts of the life of Jesus never existed for the Church apart from a living, loyal belief in him which Christians, in their own way, believed to be justified by the evidence.

x

This consideration affects our estimate of the Gospel writers. The great portrait painter divines what is hidden from the detached recorder. His gift of keen sympathy with his subject enables him to see deeper into the personality of his subject than is possible for the impartiality of the technical observer or objective critic. An eminent philosopher used to tell his students that "admiration and love often anticipate the intelligence, and the heart may obscurely realize the presence of a power which the mind cannot measure."[19]

---

[19] Dr. Edward Caird repeated this in his *Evolution of Theology in the Greek Philosophers* (vol. ii, p. 352) ; see Joachim Wach in *Das Verstehen* (vol. ii, pp. 7f.) and in *Die Religion in Geschichte und Gegenwart* (2d ed., pp. 1570-1573).

This was a hard saying for undergraduates who half a century ago sought first the kingdom of intelligence, in theory if not in practice. The words sounded like an intrusion of emotion upon knowledge. But the hearers grew up to find that this axiom was a commonplace of serious psychological and historical research, and that it applied to the study of Jesus as well as to investigation into the commanding figures of classical literature and history. The more strenuously people take the right and the duty of examining the text and texture of the relevant Christian documents by the best available methods of objective inquiry, if only to guard against a sentimental or dilettante interpretation which reads into them private idiosyncrasies, the more imperative it becomes, as recent historians warn us, to treat these documents as religious writings which demand a certain affinity between the interpreter and what he is analyzing or expounding. Otherwise the treatment is apt to be one-sided or superficial, for all its ingenuity. Nearly all the beliefs that inspire and control life go beyond what can be proved by abstract argument and neat reconstruction, whether they relate to the past or to living men and women in the present.

In short, the writers of the Gospels are not mere recorders; they may be compared to great portrait painters, who never attempt to put on their canvas all that they see at the moment, but feel free to take liberties in selecting, arranging, and coloring details in order to bring out the significance of the subject as it appeals to them. The painter may be depicting what others have already painted, but each seeks to portray the enduring meaning that the face or figure has for himself. None aims at photographic accuracy or completeness. One will see in his subject what others pass by, largely because no two exactly agree in choosing the precise details which bring out the whole that dominates the details and yet does not exist apart from them. Such portraits, as Lord Haldane once argued, "may vary in expression and yet be true, for the characteristic of what is alive and intelligent and spiritual is that it may have many expressions, all of which may be true"; so that, to broaden the argument, "just as there may be several portraits, all of superlative excellence, while differing in details and even in their presentation of actual features, so there may be histories equal in value but differing in a similar fashion."[20] The New Testament literature has sketched several interpretations of Jesus. But these interpretations are not so many private fictions and fantasies; they mean that there is something or someone far from commonplace to be interpreted. Their very variety is occasioned by the richness of their common theme, especially as it turns out to have been a creative personality.

The overwhelming impression made by Jesus upon his immediate followers and their successors is brought out by the various attempts to realize the meaning of

[20] *The Meaning of History,* pp. 7-8, 33.

his appearance. These at first were occasioned by the desire to lay emphasis upon the identity of Jesus with the glorified Christ. It took several forms, colored by contemporary ideas of the supernatural. One is reflected in a primitive story of the ascension, where the eleven apostles, looking up to heaven, are assured that "this same Jesus" (he and no other) "who is taken up from you into heaven, shall so come as you have seen him go." It was the naïve hope of many in the first generation that they would live to recognize him when he returned in triumph; whatever changes might take place during the interval, he would be the same to the eyes of faith and love as he had been on earth. No phantasm or supernatural *revenant* from the unseen world was to revisit the faithful. Indeed one prophet sternly put the other side of this expectation by reminding his readers that the Lord would be recognized by those who had murdered him and, as they imagined, had finally got rid of him as a dangerous nuisance to the nation. "Behold, he cometh on the clouds, and every eye shall see him, even those who pierced him." This realism was accompanied by a more heartening outlook, as when one writer encouraged his readers of the second generation to believe that at the end the Lord would be manifested to complete what he had himself begun in the lives of his adherents. "Beloved, we are the children of God now; what we are to be is not apparent yet, but we do know that when he appears," when God is disclosed fully through Christ in

the future, "we shall be like him, for we are to see
him as he is," in the complete reality of his presence
and person, freed from all human limitations. Christ
is what he is, it is implied; the unknown future contains the promise that his transforming power will
come into play still more effectively than it has yet
been able to do. When Christina Rossetti sang her
lyrical apostrophe to the apostle Paul—

> "To start thee on thy outrunning race
> Christ shows the splendor of his face;
> What will that face of splendor be
> When at the end he welcomes thee?"—

she was only echoing a belief that runs through the
New Testament literature, where it takes several forms.
Even apart from the short, eager expectation of a
speedy return, it thrilled the Church with the conviction that to be the same was not to be stagnant. To
preach Jesus was in one sense to say the last word.
There could not be a series of Christs; whatever
people might do in Vishnu land, Christians looked for
no fresh avatar. Once and for all, in his service and
sacrifice, the Lord had revealed the Father, fulfilling
the highest hopes and promises of the earlier revelation
to Israel. Catholic Christians with one consent saw in
their Lord the climax of the best in the Old Testament; indeed they now read their sacred book in the
light of Jesus Christ, just as they saw him in the light
of the far past to which he was the clue. Yet to preach

Jesus was also to say the first word about the life which was now opening up for human faith. The Church was conscious of a regenerating power, and as that force or Spirit, like all forms of power, revealed itself in overcoming obstacles within a resisting medium of inertia and dullness, they came to appreciate more fully than ever what the incarnation had meant. A new world of experience and opportunity spread before them, with the living Christ to inspire them. Yet it was the same Jesus as of old, realized by the faithful in their common service of the one God and Father.

Part Two

INSIDE THE CHURCH AS WELL AS OUTSIDE, MEN AND women are at times disposed to agree with A. E. Housman, "We have to sing, 'My soul doth magnify the Lord,' when what we want to sing is, 'O that my soul could find a Lord to magnify.'" This hesitation or uncertainty may be in part the fault of the very Church which is doing its best to magnify the Lord God. The best may not be good enough, and it is never good enough .if it represents the Lord sending Jesus as an ordinary individual into the world, or if it allows him to become little more than a conventional vague figure of the supernatural world, mainly important for some plan of salvation, but more important for what he did than for what he was and is. In either way the divine humanity of Christ is misrepresented. At the one extreme, Christ's humanity is admitted, but all that is divine in him is attributed to the speculations and naïve reverence of followers who deified his person and sacrificed Jesus to the Christ. At the other extreme, Jesus the Son of man almost evaporates in the second Person of the blessed Trinity, who indeed lived on earth for a few years but who, apart from theological metaphysics, is practically unknown or vital to the faithful except in some rite of worship. It is no wonder that,

59

with such presuppositions, the faith of the Magnificat fails to satisfy the mind and heart. Even when the Saviour is truly honored, as in the evangelical revival that stirred England during last century, it may be without due recognition of the Jesus who lives for us in the Gospels. And even when the Jesus of history is depicted, it does not follow that he is preached or studied in vital connection with anything that can be called a gospel in the Christian sense of the term. Historians have often noticed the significant reasons why Luther resented some popular preaching of the Roman Church in Germany upon the historical Jesus. In his pamphlet on the Freedom of a Christian, he protested, "It is not enough, it is not Christian, to preach the works of Christ, his life and words, merely in a historical manner, in the sense that they once occurred, as if knowledge of these facts would suffice by way of example for the conduct of life, though such is the practice of those who today are taken to be our best preachers. Much less does it suffice to keep silence about Christ altogether and to teach, instead of him, the laws of men and decrees of the fathers. Not a few also are preaching Christ and eagerly reading about him in order to stir up men's emotions to sympathy with Christ and to anger against the Jews, and suchlike childish, effeminate hysteria. Rather should Christ be so preached that faith in him may be firm to the end, that he may be not only Christ but a Christ for you and for me." It was bad enough to say little or nothing

60

about Christ. But to preach about him as a remote figure, in a sort of impressionistic fashion, or to use the gospel story in order to work up sentimental emotions and even anti-Semitism, as some Germans were doing in the beginning of the sixteenth century, was still worse.

Three centuries have not seen the disappearance of these three wrong methods of preaching. But they have seen, especially of late, a certain dissatisfaction with the theology of the two natures in Christ, which Luther could still use effectively, as he preached the Lord rightly. "The Word was God. . . . And the Word became flesh," simply means "The Word was divine. . . . And the Word became human." The Nicene faith, in the Chalcedon definition, was intended to conserve both of these truths against theories that failed to present Jesus as truly God and truly man; it was not an attempt to define characteristics which cannot be sharply distinguished. But that age had no clear idea of what we mean by personality, and its language about substance and natures was more appropriate to things than to personal life. Hence a desire has arisen to express the truth in more adequate psychological terms, which will not suggest a dual personality or an unnatural blending of the divine and the human in the Lord's character.

i

This would be to do what the early centuries tried

to do, with the New Testament in their hands. They did it in more ways than one. The theological statement was accompanied by a persistent response to the living Spirit of Jesus in church life. The conviction that Christianity was Christianity as it worshipped God through Jesus Christ pervaded more than the twenty-seven books or tracts which were finally included in the canon. The literature of the early Church shows abundant traces of such a faith. The one primitive exception is a large book of revelations and parables composed by a prophetic teacher of the Roman Church, called Hermas. His *Shepherd* is second-rate literature, but it had enormous influence on the moral praxis of the early Church. The perplexing thing is that while Hermas has plenty to say about angels, and while he refers once or twice to the Son of God, though generally in an austere, aloof rôle, for some reason the name of Jesus or Christ is absent from the confused theology of his pages. On the other hand, the divine humanity of the Lord inspired the monastic movement in the third century. When Anthony, the young Copt, started this enterprise, he was roused by a word of Jesus, not by any words about Jesus; "If thou wilt be perfect, go and sell that thou hast and give to the poor, and come and follow me." The very fact that Jerome, toward the end of the fourth century, led his monastic adherents away from the deteriorating atmosphere of Rome to the Holy Land, did as much to stimulate a vivid sense of the historic Jesus as had been accomplished by the devotion of Queen Helena to the sacred sites in Palestine. Similarly it was partly due to the awakening of interest in Palestine by the Crusades, that Francis of Assisi became inspired to think realistically of Jesus. What exasperated many of his fellow churchmen in the sixteenth century was that Erasmus revealed the New Testament "philosophy of Christ,"[1] as he called it, and exposed monks and friars, as well as theologians, who were either relegating Jesus to a second place of importance or degrading his religion.

The revivals and reforms of the Church have commonly been due to a sudden consciousness that Jesus Christ had been forgotten or undervalued in the very Church which bore his name, "As in the earth's core, so in the core of every vital religion," Andrew Lang wrote in his biography of Lockhart, "lives a fire; on occasion it will break the crust of decent routine and will excite the terror or the laughter of the 'rational.' Yet without this fire there would be no spiritual life, and without its volcanic outbursts there would be none of life's cleansing and renewal." Over and again this upsetting ferment has been stirred by nothing so much as by a return to the record of Jesus in his earthly life. Theologies have had to be recast, as a result. Stereotyped traditions of thought and of practice have been disturbed by a thrill of reality and fresh enter-

---

[1] Henry Glarean, a young scholar and schoolmaster at Basle, for example, wrote to thank him (September 5th, 1516) for this; "Above all the benefits you bestowed on me, you always taught me to know Christ, and more than that, to imitate Him, to reverence Him, to love Him."

63

prise, and even confronted with an appeal to Jesus Christ against their declensions. " 'Pilate said to him, What is truth? And when he had said this, he went out.' It is a sad pity for the human race that Pilate went out, instead of waiting for the answer." So Voltaire, in the *Dictionnaire Philosophique*. Since Pilate, others have been more curious and patient about the meaning of truth in connection with Jesus Christ, though it cannot be said their reports have always heartened mankind. But Jesus did say one word to Pilate which it is a sad pity if the Church is too preoccupied to ponder. On the eve of the Vatican Council in 1870, when Professor Mozley of Oxford preached his great sermon on "My kingdom is not of this world," he began: "This is a text which has, as it were, looked at the Church ever since the Church was founded. It is like an eye fixed upon her, from which she cannot escape; she has in times past thought she has escaped from it, but that eye has been upon her, and it is looking upon her now, when the Church stands face to face again with Christ in the judgment-hall, saying, 'My kingdom is not of this world.' " When the New Testament is regarded as a varied witness to the same, commanding place of Jesus Christ in the revelation and realization of God's will on earth, one of its functions is to challenge the very Church which retains it. The appeal to the New Testament has not indeed been invariably wise, any more than the neglect of it. But the conviction of what the Lord is in the gospel has been repeatedly brought home to Christians, often through stern experiences; it has broken through misconceptions, conventionalism, and indifference, rousing a better conscience in many circles and reviving the central truths of the faith, in belief and practice, when they were in danger of being either narrowed or evaporated. "Behold, I stand at the door and knock. If—." This is at once the disturbing crisis and the perennial hope of every generation. All depends upon the human response to the Lord of life.

But here and there, now and then, preoccupations and contemporary influences have relegated Jesus to a secondary position in his religion. In the chapel of the archbishop's palace at Ravenna, the place of honor in a set of marvelous mosaics, dating from the fifth and sixth centuries, was occupied originally by a striking figure of our Lord, with a thin cross carried on his right shoulder, and in his hand a book or scroll bearing the words, "Ego sum via et veritas et vita." This represented the genuine catholic faith of the undivided Church, that the center of revelation lay in him who was the way, the truth, and the life. But the focus was altered before long. This dominant figure of the Lord was put into a corner, to make room for the present occupant of the central position, "an eleventh-century mosaic Madonna with a saint of the same date on each side"[2] of her.

---

[2] *Life and Letters of F. J. A. Hort,* vol. ii, p. 351.

There is another significant trace of this sub-Christian tendency in popular medieval religion, indicated not by art but by literature. Frederic Harrison, in his "New Calendar of Great Men," hailed the "Divina Commedia" as "the foundation of the Bible to be." But if so, this new Bible will require to be enriched beyond the limits of a positivist ideal, provided that it is designed to reach Christians. For one of the disconcerting features in Dante's masterpiece is the casual and scanty place assigned to Jesus Christ. His name is never mentioned except twice in the closing cantos of the "Paradiso," and there only indirectly in quotations (xxv. 33, xxxi. 107). Naturally there are one or two allusions elsewhere to his life on earth; but while in the Latin prose of the De Monarchia Dante wrote directly about that life in order to illustrate a political thesis of the Church and the world, in the poem he prefers medieval symbols like those of the Gryphon, half eagle and half lion, drawing the chariot of the Church, or of the pelican which generously gives its own blood to feed its young. Thomas Aquinas in his hymn could hail the Lord as "pie pelicane, Jesu domine," but there is no "Jesu domine" in Dante's references. For him, as for those who produced the splendid art of Chartres Cathedral, personal devotion was more warmly kindled by the Virgin queen of heaven than by the Lord Jesus Christ.

The same unconcern about Jesus is to be traced later, notably in a minor figure like Georges de Brébeuf,

the seventeenth-century translator of Lucan. He was a
humanist but a devout member of the Roman Church,
far from being a deist. Yet it is disquieting to find
that his devotional poetry in the *Entretiens Solitaires*
shows not the least interest in the Gospels. It is the
Virgin, not her Son, who appeals to this French pietist.
He enjoys a Christianity without Christ. And for other
reasons a similar tendency emerges in other communions of the Church. Burns, for example, was not
a deist like Pope. He was a much more religious man.
It is true that while the Scots poet wrote as indignantly
about some Calvinistic ministers as Dante had done
about Roman churchmen, his genius was essentially
lyrical; it was not his vocation to write a long poem
upon the world and time from the point of view of
theology. Still, when we overhear him occasionally
touching the inwardness of religion in his day with
sympathy and insight, as in "The Cottar's Saturday
Night," it must be admitted that he does not show any
vivid interest in Jesus Christ. The reason may be that
the Jesus of the Gospels was not a commanding figure
in the type of Church Christianity which Burns happened to encounter and to deride. Also he may have
had a natural reticence which hindered him from writing about what meant more to him than his letters or
poems disclose. Yet the fact remains; he had more
interest in the prophets and tales of the Old Testament, with their emphasis on justice, charity, and duty,
than in the specific revelation of the New Testament.

"I see no trace in Burns's poetry that Christ had any meaning to him," an English critic wrote; "I see nothing but a fine theism." The verdict of Stopford Brooke is not unjustified. So far as the genius of Burns expressed itself in anything he wrote about religion, it produced little more than an uninspiring theism.

In all these cases the official creed was truer than the popular religion of the Church. All the three men mentioned belonged to churches where Jesus "born of the Virgin Mary" was hailed as the supreme Saviour. "There is no salvation by anyone else, nor even a second Name under heaven appointed for us men and our salvation." The very adoration of Mary was a by-product of faith in the Son of God. But the religious experience, or lack of experience, shows how the Jesus of actual life had become less and other than the Jesus of the confession.

ii

The catholicism of the early Church was free from such aberrations. Yet even then the divine humanity of the Lord was not always presented with adequate effect. It is generally agreed that between the third and the sixth centuries there was a deflection of thought[3] in the Church's failure to appreciate what

---

[3] This has been recently restated by Dr. R. V. Sellers in *Two Ancient Christologies* (London, 1940) The arguments of this excellent essay should be read in the light of data supplied from various angles in Dr. G. L. Prestige's *God in Patristic Thought* (London, 1936), and in Jules Gross's *La Divinisation du Chrétien d'après les Pères Grecs* (Paris, 1938), along with Professor Creed's *The Divinity of Jesus Christ* (1938).

the great Antioch school of exegesis maintained by its
stress on a literal, historical interpretation, as opposed
to the allegorical methods of the Alexandrian. The
former, no doubt, was compromised by the appeal to it
made by some who differed from the Athanasian faith,
and who sometimes represented the character of Jesus
as a human achievement rather than as a divine revelation; but the better Antiochenes upheld the need
for a direct unembarrassed view of the historical Christ,
who had moral and mental growth, who had suffered
and struggled, as the New Testament exhibited his real
and complete humanity. The Nicene creed had the
same object, it is true; those responsible for its composition had sought to maintain the faith of the New
Testament in the full manhood of the historic Christ.
Yet from the fourth century onward, the New Testament evidence for his human personality was not
always faced satisfactorily. The "two-natures" formula
was originally intended to conserve belief in the real
humanity of Jesus Christ against contemporary speculation which seemed to impair or endanger this saving
truth. To some of us the catholic faith came through
the simple affirmation of the Westminster Shorter Cate-
chism that "the Lord Jesus Christ, being the eternal
Son of God, became man, and so was, and continueth
to be, God and man in two distinct natures, and one
person, forever." But whether the Nicene faith came
through the Nicene creed or not, the unity of God has
been safeguarded as well as the reality of the Saviour

Son, in all catholic communions of the West and the East. The drawback was that when the Gospels came to be interpreted in terms of this creed, the tendency of some early thinkers was to represent Jesus now speaking as God, now as man, until an air of unreality crept into exegesis. Whatever may be thought of the Nicene statement, it led to an insufficient appreciation of the apostolic evidence that Jesus invariably acted and spoke within the limitations of his divine manhood, and that he was one person, not possessed of a twofold personality. This result was not foreseen. It might have been prevented, as some wise Christians pled. Thus Bishop Eusebius of Caesarea laid before the Nicene council the creed of his own church, which after "suffered," in the article on Christ, read "who lived his life among men." One creed of Syrian Christians, preserved in the Apostolic Constitutions, also added, after the virgin birth, the affirmation that the Lord "lived a holy life according to the laws of God his Father." It is to be regretted that some phrase of this kind was not admitted to the Nicene creed, for such words witness to the divine humanity of Christ as the apostolic testimony of the New Testament preserves it. But the current was running so strongly toward emphasis on the divinity of the Son that the cardinal features of his life on earth, so far as the official theology was concerned, came to be regarded as the cradle and the cross, till his moral character seemed of less importance.

70

Apart from the theologians, this did not much matter to the general body of Christians, who repeated the Apostles' Creed and sang the Te Deum, where no such technical phrases perplexed them, as they praised the Son of God. We may agree with Dryden

"That many have been saved, and many may,
  Who never heard this question brought in play.
  The unlettered Christian, who believes in gross,[4]
  Plods on to heaven and ne'er is at a loss."

It has always been so. But the time comes when Christians are not all unlettered. Once the New Testament is put into their hands, they demand to hear this question raised. Unless some honest answer is offered, they may be as much at a loss as the native convert in Kipling's *Plain Tales From the Hills,* who left the mission station and went back to her pagan beliefs, crying,

"To my own gods I go,
  It may be they will give me greater ease
  Than your cold Christ and tangled Trinities."

It is not the purpose of this essay to suggest any fresh formula for the divine nature of Christ, but simply to indicate how the historical study of the New Testament may serve to prevent an interpretation of the Lord which leaves him cold and unreal. His divine humanity is our ground for believing in his identity. The New Testament on a fair reading attests this.

---

[4] That is, in general, without attending to the minutiae of his creed, or to learned definitions of Christ's person.

71

But in five directions, at least, the records have been and are being understood in such a way that the divine humanity does not make its full impression upon the mind.

iii

The Church read more into "ecce homo" than Pilate had intended. It was not in scorn or pity, but in deep gratitude and wonder, that they hailed their Lord as man. Sometimes it is an instinctive cry, sometimes a protest against the idea that a spiritual Christ could be detached from a historical Jesus, but invariably it shows men looking at One who had been for them a real man and not a transient or phantom appearance on earth. "There is one mediator between God and man, the man Christ Jesus." "Jesus of Nazareth was a man accredited by God, who raised him from the dead; death could not hold him." "For since by man came death, by man also came resurrection from the dead." "One who was in all points tempted like as we are, yet without sin." Or, as an early Christian sermon of the second century[5] put it, "when the Almighty sent him, it was as a king sending his son; he sent him as king, he sent him as God, he sent him as man; it was to save and persuade that he sent him, not using compulsion, for compulsion does not belong to God." Nothing could be more explicit. The divine Jesus, in whatever sense he was thought to be divine, was be-

---

[5] *Epistle to Diognetus,* vii. 3.

lieved to have lived a true human life. He was no
angel. His life had not been a mere theophany, flash-
ing into the human sphere, apart from a real character
and destiny. The full disclosure of God's nature required One who was "the man, Christ Jesus." Yet in
endeavoring to find and exalt Jesus as the Christ of
God some, for various reasons, have almost lost sight
of the man.

In our own day this one-sided tendency has been
fostered not so much by an apprehension that the spiritual is blurred or compromised if it is in close contact with the realities of flesh and blood, as (a) by a
desire to detach religion from the sphere of relativity
and historical uncertainty. Facing the skepticism of
historical proof, for example, Hegel found himself
much more at home among ideas than among events
and personalities, which he preferred to use as illustra-
tions of phases in a dialectic process. His spirit affected
a writer like Strauss, as the latter wrote his biography
of Jesus; a great individual was reckoned to be little
more than the embodiment or representation of a general idea, and inevitably Jesus was belittled. Or again
(b), the gospel of Jesus may be depicted as a shattering
challenge thrown down to men on earth. While this is
at least more accurate than the sketch of a Galilean
idyl, it is none the less untrue to the full scope of the
historical facts. Then (c) orthodox theology itself,
both Greek and Latin, has sometimes tended to treat
the record of what Jesus actually experienced on earth

as appearance rather than reality, till his human nature became chiefly essential for the purpose of the sacrifice on Calvary. Finally (d) there is a critical approach to the Lord's life which eliminates nearly all the vivid personal details as reflections of what later generations came to see in him rather than as original data of his personality. The common feature in all such schemes is that a certain impression of unreality is produced, even, indeed especially, by some who believe in the reality of the incarnation, from Clement of Alexandria and Hilary of Poitiers onward. There has been hesitation to accept the true humanity of Jesus Christ as Gospels and Epistles depicted it, and a habit of interpreting certain sayings in a non-realistic sense. Jesus, for example, did not ask questions because he needed information, and he did not eat because he needed food; all this was only meant to show that he was a real person. Did Luke describe how he "advanced in wisdom and favor with God"? It was not really so; he simply behaved as if it were so, Anselm explains, going on to interpret "he learned obedience by the things which he suffered" by saying that Jesus acted in such a way as to make others learn this truth.[6]

iv

One of the first points at which the manhood of Jesus came to be seriously imperilled, was in connection with sayings which guaranteed his real humanity but at the

_____
[6] *Cur Deus Homo,* i. 9, 10.

74

same time appeared to suggest limitations in his knowledge of the present and the future. The most famous was his authentic word, "No one knows anything of that day or hour, not even the angels in heaven, not even the Son, but only the Father."[7] Such was the original form of the saying. But, soon after the days of Origen, the words "not even the Son" were often left out of Matthew's text and even occasionally out of Mark's. There was an uneasy feeling that they were an embarrassing admission which did not harmonize with faith in his divine perfection. During the Athanasian controversy they were frequently explained away by recourse to subtle deductions from the dogma of the two natures in Jesus. Athanasius himself is not entirely happy in his treatment of the words. Later on, some like Ambrose of Milan suspected that they were an Arian gloss, while those who ventured to take the saying in its full meaning were attacked by Athanasians, who flung the taunt of "Arian" at them no less recklessly and no more sensibly than men today in a different field glory in "Aryan." Augustine was one of the scholars who were driven to plead that while Jesus did know when the last day was to come, he neither could nor would reveal it to his hearers. This satisfied

---

[7] Mark xiii. 32, Matthew xxiv. 36. The earliest textual phenomena are discussed in Canon Streeter's *Four Gospels* (pp. 549f.), the early patristic views in H. Schlingensiepin's *Die Wunder des Neuen Testamentes: Wege und Abwege ihrer Deutung in der alten Kirche bis zur Mitte des fünften Jahrhunderts* (pp. 194f.), and later opinions are included in Jules Lebreton's *Histoire du dogme de la Trinité des Origines au Concile du Nicée*, vol. i. Note C (Eng. tr. pp. 417-452).

Aquinas. Even Father Lagrange,[8] who will have nothing to do with the official theory of the two natures as a clue to the saying, practically relapses on a view like Augustine's ("The Son knows, but he is not commissioned to impart such knowledge"), although he confesses that such exegesis may appear evasive, "trop subtile et un peu semblable à une échappatoire." It is refreshing to read Calvin's straightforward remark, in his *Commentaire sur La Concordance ou Harmonie composée de trois évangélistes,* that if Christ as man did not know the last day, this is no more derogatory to his nature than the fact that he was mortal. To interpret the saying otherwise than in line with the fact that Jesus grew in wisdom as well as in stature, that he was often taken by surprise, and that he had to ask for information like an ordinary being, is to be zealous for his divine nature at some expense to the truth of his humanity; however difficult it may be to state the mystery of both in adequate terms, the relevant texts should not be subjected to any forced or artificial treatment.

There is a perplexing passage in the story of Lazarus, which indicates that even within the New Testament traditions the difficulty emerges. According to the narrative of the Fourth Gospel, Jesus asked the mourners where they had buried his friend, and on going to the grave he wept. Both statements are perfectly natural as they stand. Jesus did not know where

---

[8] In his *L'Evangile selon S. Marc* (5th ed., 1929).

the grave was, and he was not above feeling strong emotion in contact with death. But it sounds less natural to be told that after the boulder had been rolled aside from the tomb, and when "Jesus lifting his eyes to heaven said, Father, I thank thee for listening to me" (i. e., calmly sure that the miracle was now to take place, in response to some unrecorded prayer), he instantly added, "I knew thou wouldest always listen to me, but I spoke" (i. e., I have thanked thee aloud) "on account of the crowd around, that they might believe thou hast sent me." The author or an editor here makes the Lord explain to the Father, not that he had prayed, but that he was now putting his gratitude into words in order to impress bystanders with the significance of the miracle which was about to transpire. The explanation resembles that of the thunder peal in a subsequent story, but it is specially artificial here; it appears to make the Lord practice the devotional life with a view to effect. The pragmatism which led the author to represent his Jesus as controversial and argumentative in certain sections (e. g., in chapters v-vii) has slightly blurred the divine humanity of the Son by conveying the impression that in a moment of divine communion with God he could think of how best to edify bystanders. And this misled many early patristic interpreters, who denied that the first question really implied ignorance of the locality of the tomb. In a desire to emphasize the divinity of the Lord, men from the time of Hilary declared that the

question meant no more than God's question to Adam, "Where art thou?" Jesus must have known perfectly well where the tomb was. Indeed, they continued, Jesus did not even need to pray for the miracle; he merely prayed in order to teach men how and why to pray. So disconcerting was this passage that we find schoolmen, from John of Damascus to Aquinas, urging that when the Lord lifted up his eyes to heaven, it was not that he required to entreat the Father, but for the purpose of instructing men how to offer prayer. The evangelist had no such ideas, however. Here, as elsewhere, for all his exaltation of the divine character of Jesus, living in constant, close communion with God, he notes how Jesus naturally asked people for information. What led to the unnatural interpretation of the references in the present story was the rather unhappy addition of the Lord's comment on the reason why he gave thanks in public, as though he prayed in order to be heard or overheard by men.

v

The divine humanity of Jesus is impaired when justice is not done to his prayer-life. It is one thing to say that the Gospels were not written to depict an ideally religious life for adherents of the Lord to follow, or to exhibit the inward character of Jesus as a man of God; it is another thing to infer that allusions to Jesus praying are upon the whole secondary and unauthentic. This is to throw things out of focus. It is impossible to

separate what God did through Jesus from what Jesus was and did in relation to God and man during his earthly ministry, as though details about the latter must have been relatively unimportant to those who remembered him. Any literary analysis which eliminates all mention of the prayers of Jesus from what is supposed to be the earliest strata of tradition, betrays an error of perspective. The first disciples knew that as a man of God their Lord had prayed for himself as well as for others. He was expected to pray. When children were once brought to him, it was that he might lay his hands on them and pray. He prayed on the night before he chose the twelve, and once after a hard day's work. He taught his followers to pray by his example, as well as by his instructions. It was as they watched him praying that they ventured to ask him for guidance in prayer. According to Luke, he was praying at his baptism, before the crucial confession at Caesarea Philippi, and also at the transfiguration on the hillside. To rule out such allusions is to rewrite history in the interests of an ideology, not to interpret it.

But the first mention of his prayers in Mark is specially significant. After a long and surprisingly successful day of healing and exorcising at Capernaum, he rose before dawn and slipped away to a lonely spot in the country. He was praying there when Simon and the others at last discovered him. They reproached him for abandoning his popularity in the town. But he had been praying for divine guidance. Was he to

79

allow his sudden local fame as a thaumaturgist to inter-
fere with his mission of preaching far and wide? The
prayer was for light and strength in view of his vocation. Surely nothing could be more natural than this
recourse to prayer, and nothing more likely than that
the disciples should recollect an incident which cannot
fail to have impressed them. For some reason Luke, in
recording the story, left out the mention of prayer, but
this was not due to any tendency to minimize prayer
in the life of Jesus, for elsewhere he introduces prayer
at special moments of the ministry. No text of Mark
ever left out the allusion to prayer here. It was reserved for a presbyter of Antioch, Victor, to explain
away such prayers by declaring that Jesus merely
offered them by way of example or formally, not
because he needed to pray, but because he desired to
instruct his followers.

Unfortunately, Victor was not the last to take this
bypath of mistaken reverence. Traces of such patristic
evasion still linger in connection with the moving
account of the Lord's prayers in the garden of Gethsemane, as recorded in the first three Gospels, which is
paralleled by the allusion in Hebrews to "the days of
his flesh, when with bitter cries and tears he offered
prayers and supplications to Him who was able to save
him from death." Here patristic misinterpretation
and modern criticism join hands. The "cries and
tears" may be a romantic touch added by the writer,
but he at least intended them to be real; he never

80

meant, as Aquinas thought he did, to suggest that Jesus wept for the wicked world, not for himself in any personal anguish. The Gethsemane prayers for strength to accept the Father's will were wrung out of an intensely human shrinking from death. No one in primitive Christendom ever imagined that the Gethsemane story was composed in order to describe the heroic faith of Jesus, but it is incredible that the tradition was no more than an edifying later transcript of what had originally been a tale told in order to contrast the courageous faith of Jesus and his agonized resignation to the divine will, with an indifference to the ordeal on the part of his disciples. It is fairly clear that some traits in the Lucan version reflect a heightened emphasis, due to the interests of the Church. But no such factor created the tradition as we have it, that here, as at other crucial moments, Jesus prayed for himself as well as for his followers. Nor are the allusions in Hebrews the result of a writer weaving texts from the psalms about a good man in agony, into an imaginative picture of Jesus at prayer in the crisis.[9] Later on, the Church indeed used to find a biography of Jesus in the Psalter. Even as early as the New Testament itself, citations from the psalms occur in Gospels and Epistles where the life and character of Jesus are depicted. By the second century, when some Christians read a line from the ninety-sixth psalm, "Say

---

[9] So, e. g., R. Bultmann, *Geschichte der Synoptischen Tradition* (2d ed.), pp. 288f., and M. Dibelius, *From Tradition to Gospel*, pp. 211f.

among the nations that the Lord has entered on his reign," they added "from the tree" or cross, sure that this must have been the original text. In the homily of Hebrews, the writer himself cites one psalm to prove the final nature of Christ the Son, and another to illustrate his eternal priesthood. But no such method is followed in the reference to Gethsemane. The correct interpretation of the Gethsemane tradition was given long ago by Calvin with characteristic insight and honesty in his *Concordance,* where[10] he denied that the cry of Jesus could be regarded as anything but a real prayer. While Christ had no confused emotions to distract him, like those to which human beings may be subject in an emergency, yet "strong grief did take from him the immediate recollection of God's will, so that for the moment he did not recall that to suffer death was the condition on which he was sent to be the redeemer of mankind." This goes to the heart of the matter. It was a timely correction of the tradition laid down by John of Damascus and by Aquinas that the prayers of Jesus at the tomb of Lazarus and in Gethsemane were simply intended to be a lesson for the Church. Recent exponents of Greek and Roman theology like Dr. Karl Adam, in the fifth chapter of his book on *The Son of God,* and Dr. Sergius Bulgakov in *The Wisdom of God* (pp. 135f.), have indeed repudi-

---

[10] On Matthew xxvi. 39. The services rendered to this truth by Calvin, for all his limitations, are discussed by Max Dominicé in *L'humanité de Jésus d'Après Calvin* (Paris, 1933).

ated this interpretation, the latter especially admitting
that the Son of God "underwent all the limitations and
infirmities of human life. Times and seasons had their
effect upon his life. He was subject to every human
propensity which does not involve sin; he continually
prayed to his Father in heaven as God." The Epistle
to the Hebrews, which stresses this truth, has been curi-
ously embarrassing to many open-minded thinkers of
the Roman Communion, from Cardinal Cajetan to
Baron von Hügel; they thought it inadequate as a testimony to the Lord's divinity. But its emphasis on the
Lord's divine humanity in prayer and in suffering is a
corrective to inferences which might be, as they have
been, drawn from the tendency of a document like the
Fourth Gospel to bring out the divinity by omitting
direct references to the Lord in prayer, and by suggest-
ing at several points that he was too divine and omnis-
cient to be influenced by advice from others, or surprised by anything in the human scene.

When catholic interpreters[11] imply that Jesus prayed
in part if not entirely by way of example, or in order
to impress people with his reality in the flesh, and when
some practitioners of Form criticism maintain that,
while Jesus may have prayed, his first followers could
not have taken any interest in this, the recovery of a
true perspective depends on the recognition that refer-

---

[11] Hilary of Poitiers, in his book on the Trinity and elsewhere (e.g., on
Psalm liv. 3), was the leading spirit; he was misled by his Alexandrian
masters.

ences to his prayer-life are embedded in the earliest
strata of tradition, that, even when they are later, they
are upon the whole in character, and that all attest his
natural humanity. Had Jesus not offered real prayer,
which is the highest inward action of the human soul,
the record of his humanity would have been imperfect.
The allusions to prayer do not belong to any penumbra
of reverence, nor to a purely biographical vein of pious
legend. It is inconceivable that they would have been
absent from any memories of his life. A thoughtful
man like Dr. John McLeod Campbell[12] once wrote to
a friend about the religious value of such gospel reminiscences. Speaking of Luke's record that Jesus "went
out into the mountain to pray, and continued all night
in prayer to God," he confessed that this "has been
more frequently present to my thoughts both for re-
buke and for guidance, than the practice and preaching
of Saint Paul." McLeod Campbell could not be satisfied with the apostle's injunction alone. "His exhorta-
tion to 'pray without ceasing' has been to me one with
our Lord's speaking a parable that men ought always to
pray and not to faint." Such an instinctive recourse
to the Gospels for aid in the practice of prayer does not
explain why stories about Jesus praying would be created by the primitive Church; it explains why from the
first they were cherished and recorded. It also involves
that these prayers of Jesus must have been real, not
uttered for any educational purpose, as is implied by

[12] *Memorials,* vol. ii, p. 37.

patristic interpretations which exploit the references instead of expounding them. For example, "My God, my God, why hast thou forsaken me?" is a real cry, however it may be explained. But when Leo of Rome tells his hearers that it is not a cry but a lesson, intended to give the world instruction upon the method of redemption, the words cease to be intelligible. The truth of them disappears in a theological application of the Nicene creed.

vi

While Jesus was more than a teacher, his divine humanity is not truly realized if the content and the function of his teaching are either obscured or exaggerated. It is more easy to make out the commanding significance of his instructions upon religion than any contemporary phase of religious thought in Judaism. The extant sources reveal a central and characteristic attitude of Jesus, not a kaleidoscope of various maxims, much less a record of sayings invented or adapted in order to meet later emergencies of church life. We note indeed how differences of outlook and cross-currents in the communities have affected certain items of his teaching, owing to the natural strain between the old mind and the new mind as Christianity passed through its primitive Jewish Christian phase into the larger environment of the world. But the clue to any solution of the problem raised by this interaction and vital tension is not to be found in hypotheses about a creative imagination in some groups, or in the impact of outside beliefs and practices upon a set of pious ideas more or less vaguely associated with the person of a Galilean enthusiast, who taught little or nothing of decisive importance to his original followers. The right perspective lies in seeing first of all that what he said depended on what he was, and, secondly, that community-stories could not have arisen unless he had said this or that.

Thus, when he told his disciples, "Heaven and earth will pass away, but my words will never pass away,"[13] this confident assurance did not merely refer to what he had just said or to what he was saying at the moment; "my words" are an equivalent for "my revelation" of God's will. The temple, the Torah, and all the rest of it will lapse, but not this. What is of abiding value is what he declares or announces as the divine Son in his messianic vocation; and this is the outcome of his position as the fulfiller of the divine purpose for the world. His first words in Mark's Gospel were words of authority: "The time has now come," i. e., the hour for God's reign to be inaugurated. It was more than a prophetic word; it was a word with power, spoken in the consciousness of being the chosen Son of God. His very next words to the fishermen, "Come, follow me," were not the casual utterance of a teacher picking up suitable adherents or helpers in his mission; they were the summons to a divine commission of unexampled range,

---

[13] Mark xiii. 31.

initiated by himself in the name of God. Even when a saying of this nature has been elaborated, it goes back to some actual report, transmitted by some channel of oral tradition.

To ordinary hearers in Palestine the saying, "Heaven and earth will pass away, but my words will never pass away," would serve to recall the Torah, which was God's lasting word for his people. But Jesus had already set his own word above the Torah, in criticizing the Mosaic law on divorce. So far from being a later expression of the Church's belief in their Lord as the supreme authority for faith and practice, the saying is one of the authentic utterances which account for that belief, and which helped to carry the primitive Church through the difficult period when the eager expectation of the End was mixed up with apocalyptic dreams of its imminence. It is such sayings that explain the developed views of the Fourth Gospel; they are the nucleus of the later emphasis upon Christ's person and words as the absolute expression of divine reality and revelation. Still further, they throw light on the fact that for the early Christians it was natural to think of Jesus as practically their Torah, healing and revealing, commanding and sacramental. Thus, as worship depended upon the Torah, of which it formed part, the Christian worship of God was bound up with him who was God's revelation, no longer in a book but in his person. After declaring that "Jesus Christ is the same, yesterday, today, and forever," one writer proceeds to add, "By him therefore let us offer the sacrifice of praise to God continually, from lips that celebrate his name; and do not forget beneficence and charity either. Such are the sacrifices that are acceptable to God."[14] Why "therefore"? Because Jesus Christ now is for Christians what the divine Torah had been to Jews of old, the authentic revelation which determined man's worship of God as well as his will for their lives. The temple-worship of Judaism with its material sacrifices, which rested on the fiat of the Torah, no longer existed, or at any rate it did not exist for those who had found in Jesus Christ the supreme source of forgiveness and of fellowship with God. Yet, while the sacrifice of the Lord had once for all superseded the yearly sacrifices of the ancient ritual, the person and work of Christ called for a spiritual worship with two practical sacrifices to be constantly offered, i. e., thanksgiving and beneficence. The implication is that as Jews had practiced their temple-worship because it was laid down by the Torah, so Christians must be inspired and directed to carry on their worship by Him who had become to them all that the Torah in former years had meant for the people of God. It is not only by what Jesus had said but by what he had done, or rather by what he is, that the worship and life of Christians must be regulated.

A sidelight is thrown by one writing on this relation of Jesus to the idea of the Torah. Some Semitic repre-

---

[14] Hebrews xiii. 15, 16.

sentations of the Deity in touch with his people, such
as the Face, the Name, or the Glory, were used in
primitive Christianity as well as the Word, but all,
especially that of the Face or Person, passed far beyond
their original setting when they were enlisted to set
forth the revelation of God in Jesus Christ; as when,
for example, Paul wrote that "God who said, Light
shall shine out of darkness, has shone in my heart to
illuminate men with the knowledge of God's glory in
the face of Christ." But another teacher of the primitive Church is overheard speaking of "our Lord Jesus
Christ, who is the Glory." It was evidently natural
for Saint James to think of the Lord in terms of the
divine Glory or shekinah, i. e., the embodiment of the
divine presence, as natural as it was for one of the
evangelists to recall how Jesus had said, "Where two
or three are gathered together in my name, there am
I in the midst of them." A Jewish rabbi would have
said, indeed one later rabbi did say, "Where even two
sit together and are occupied with the Torah, there
is the Glory among them," deducing this artificially
from a saying in one of the psalms.[15] But it was
especially appropriate for the Christian teacher
to think of his Lord in the Church as the Glory, since
for Christians the divine glory lay not in God's transcendent being and majesty but in his action for and
among his people. In the mind of the Church, glory

---

[15] In Pirke Aboth iii. 4, with its exegesis of Psalm lxxxii. 1 ("As it is
said, God standeth in the congregation of God").

meant pre-eminently the manifestation of God in redeeming power on earth. It was no longer a semi-personal equivalent of God's revealed presence, but embodied in the person of Jesus Christ his Son. There alone the indwelling of the divine in human nature was to be verified. And what he taught was a vital expression of this. He was mighty in word and deed. His disclosure of God was not a word coming to him, as it had been to the prophets of old. In his "I am," "I say," "I tell you truly," the note of direct authority was audible, authority carrying with it revelation, as could not be the case in Hellenistic usages of a term like "I am."

From this it follows that, while it is unhistorical to detach the ethical from the religious message of Jesus, as though the former were predominantly important for mankind, it is equally one-sided to depict or to adore his divine nature apart from what he taught about the duties and ideals of human life. As men gaze at a crucifix, they may allow their interest in the Lord's teaching to wane. Dogmatic definitions of the Trinity have their place and value, but the right focus for seeing the divine humanity of the Lord is missed when insufficient regard is paid to the moral ideal revealed in his person and teaching, on earth. As Thomas Erskine of Linlathen remarked in the beginning of his essay on "The Spiritual Order," "the power which has affected the world's history more than any other life that was ever lived in it" lay "in what He *was,* inter-

preted by what He taught." Without a full appreciation of the latter, it is not possible to verify the supreme
revelation of God's character and will in the faith of
Christendom. Not that this can be proved, in the
ordinary sense of the term, by a mere comparison of his
ethical message with other forms of religious morality.
"The truth of a moral ideal," Dr. Hastings Rashdall
urged, "is a matter of immediate judgment. The doc-
trine of a supreme revelation of God in Christ must
ultimately rest upon the affirmation of the moral consciousness that in its essential principles that moral
ideal which is most fully incarnated in Christ's teaching and life is still the truest and the highest that we
know."[16] Unless justice is done to this element of
affirmation, the apprehension of Christ's divine humanity is imperfect. It was a voice from heaven that said,
"This is my beloved Son; hear him." For some the
study of his teaching forms their first avenue to a recognition that no man ever spoke as he spoke; for all it is
essential, if they are to call him Lord as he desired to
be called. Yet it is in the personality of Christ, not in
any detached selections from his moral teaching, that
any full guarantee of ultimate truth about the faith of
the gospel is to be found.

vii

The significance of Jesus as teacher was not the creation of the later Church as it suddenly discovered that

---

[16] *God and Man*, p. 78.

it required some guidance and rules for its mission and procedure, and set to work upon constructing out of Paulinism and Hellenism and rabbinism a body of sayings which was put back into the blank life of Jesus prior to the Passion Week. Before he died, he had taught and prepared an inner group of his disciples in order to preach his message about the kingdom, thus insuring the transmission of his instructions. One of the very earliest recollections of what he said happens to belong to this special instruction: "The workman is worthy of his hire."[17] He had also taught people with authority on how to live in the new fellowship of God. If there is one feature in the primitive tradition which is reasonably certain, it is that in heralding the kingdom he not only announced the conditions of membership but predicted an imminent judgment of God which would be determined by men's attitude toward these simple, severe requirements as he had laid them down. Jesus taught the divine judgment, and taught it as one by whom God would judge mankind, primarily those who owned his authority. An early Christian homily[18] begins: "Brothers, we must think of Jesus Christ as God, as the judge of the living and the dead; we must not have poor thoughts of our salvation." For belief in the judgment sustained the conviction that life was serious, requiring not only forgiveness but faithfulness to the orders of the Lord. As the

[17] 1 Corinthians ix. 14, echoing Luke x. 7.
[18] The Second Epistle of Clement to the Corinthians.

Gospels indicate, when the Church began in the light of the resurrection to realize the new Lordship of Christ, his instructions were felt to be more momentous than ever, for the Master was now Jesus the Christ, vindicated as God's authority by the resurrection; his words of command, positive or prohibitory, were decisive for his followers. It would not be historical to say that they were oracles rather than opinions, for many were injunctions addressed to some particular situation in ordinary life. But they were commands of the Lord. Some, e. g., on matters like divorce or fasting, were slightly adapted or altered in the course of transmission. It is not always easy to determine their exact original form. Yet they were regarded as decisive for life and death.

This is one of several reasons why recent criticism has proved fatal to a favorite hypothesis in the study of the records. The idea used to be that the religion of Jesus was one thing and the religion about Jesus another; it was supposed that the text of the Gospels could be so cleared of apostolic faith in a divine Jesus Christ that the real Jesus, who simply taught a moral religion of his own, could become visible and appealing. This idea of a radical change in primitive Christianity is happily fading from the horizon. The fact that Jesus taught with an authority which criticized parts of the Torah means that his teaching had to be accepted as crucial. It implied, as we have seen, his personal authority for the faith which he proclaimed.

93

The latter cannot be whittled down to a series of pious individual opinions. He and his teaching were identified. There is not sufficient evidence to show that any group of his disciples in Galilee ever cherished his memory as that of a notable teacher rather than as a Lord to be worshipped, though emphasis might fall on one side of the truth rather than on the other. The notion of a religion taught by Jesus having been amplified or, as some theorists held, distorted by later developments into a religion about him, sounded at first attractive; it was generally connected with the rise of Paul's original version of the faith, but it proved to be untenable, as Gospels and Epistles were recognized to have been produced by the same Church, and as his judicial rôle could not be eliminated from the teaching. The common spirit within the Church, as it called men to repent, was something like this: "As God is about to pass judgment on us all, let the Christ who is to be your judge, be also your saviour." True, the reverse was put before members of the Church as a solemn warning: "Remember that your saviour is to be your judge." "Judgment must begin at the house of God." The prophet John describes God's judgment on godless pagans with their State-worship, but he begins by showing Christ's warnings as well as his encouragements to the Church; the Lord promises the faithful protection and deliverance, but he threatens any members who believe in God and are ungodly, or who are unfaithful to the truth and faith of their Lord.

94

From primitive messianic forms of expression to the interpretation in the Fourth Gospel, Jesus and judgment were vitally connected. He taught and acted as one commissioned to make men decide for God, the King and Father whom he represented, and this meant that the decision for or against him determined human destiny. No estimate of the Lord's teaching is adequate if this note is dropped or muted. Over and again it is struck, as he speaks, for individuals and for the nation. All is made to turn upon the attitude of men to his final revelation of the divine will. It was therefore a matter of vital concern to know what this will involved, by response to which man would be judged, i. e., relegated to life or death. Some expressions of this conviction were accentuated and elaborated as tradition went on; but it was present from the first in his teaching.

The evidence is not to be explained away as the mere transference of a messianic category to his person by Jewish Christian lovers of apocalyptic. He taught from the outset with unexampled authority. After his first cure in the synagogue at Capernaum, the astonished crowd exclaimed: "What ever is this?" "It's new teaching with authority behind it!" "He orders even foul spirits." "Yes, and they obey him!" So in other spheres of his instruction. The famous words, "Not everyone who says to me Lord, Lord, will get into the kingdom of heaven, but he who does the will of my Father in heaven" (or, as Luke transmits the saying, "Why call me Lord, Lord, and do not what I tell you?"), are not a later affirmation of his authority by the Church; they go back to some authentic word.[19]   To call him Lord might be an appeal for help or a claim that they belonged to his company, or, again, a devout cry in worship.   In any case the saying, intended primarily for those active in the mission, as teachers or prophets, is a protest against effusive homage which did not carry with it obedience to his commands.   He said, "This do in remembrance of me," at the Last Supper.   But he had told them already to do many things in active life. And by their response to these injunctions men were to be judged.

The very paradoxes of the Fourth Gospel bring this out.   Apparently they contrast love and judgment; in reality they unite them, for the character and the mission of Christ in love prove a judgment.   The familiar verse,

> "He did not come to judge the world,
>   He did not come to blame;
> And when we call him Saviour,
>   Then we call him by his name,"

is a half-truth.   The Jesus who said, "I have not come to judge the world, but to save the world," also said, "For judgment I am come into this world."   While "God sent not his Son into the world to judge [i. e., condemn] the world, but that the world through him

---

[19] W. Foerster, *Herr ist Jesus,* pp. 223f.

might be saved," as men accepted his revelation of the truth, still "he who will not believe in him is sentenced already, for having refused to believe in the only Son of God. And this is the sentence of condemnation, that the light has entered the world, and yet men have preferred darkness to light." In our modern phrase, Christ proves the touchstone for men. Mankind is judged by its own judgment of him on the ultimate issue. It is by obedience to him that his own followers are tested and rewarded; it is by their attitude toward him that men in general fall to be judged here and in the hereafter. The loving God is not a mere Friend behind phenomena, or an indulgent ruler, without concern for moral qualities. His self-revelation in Christ had love as its motive, but one of its inevitable consequences was judgment on deliberate disobedience and careless living. The grave conclusion to the Sermon on the Mount showed that the one safe basis for life was a full response to what Jesus had been sent to reveal, and that men would be held responsible for the side they took in the supreme issue presented by his mission. There was always awe as well as joy in the hope with which faithful Christians expected the end. "Every sin is wiped out by pardon or by punishment."[20] Tertullian's aphorism echoes the New Testament. No religion which recognizes conscience and the fact of sin fails to own that judgment is among the ultimates of life. Christians expected "after death

---

[20] *De Pudicitia* ii : omne delictum aut venia dispungit aut poena.

the judgment," when their Lord was to judge man, not to be judged along with men. It is not always realized how significant this conviction was for their conception of his character.

From an early period efforts were made to soften or obliterate the function of Jesus as judge. Marcion's brilliant perversion of the gospel was the first and the most thoroughgoing movement in this direction; the austere moral elements of God's eternal justice were cut out of the picture as Jewish intrusions, and the saviour was glorified at the expense of the judge. Instead of retribution, evils like cruelty and treachery merely received a few disapproving words from the deity. Later, at the opposite extreme, some circles of Latin medievalism produced a popular religion in which the thought of Christ as saviour was almost lost in the overwhelming conception of Christ as the final judge. When his teaching and human person were comparatively neglected, he was viewed as the inflicter of severe doom, from whose sentence the one refuge of mankind lay in the merciful Mother of God, to whom sinners appealed as the only hope of inducing her Son to mitigate his hard sentence on the race. Instead of seeing in Jesus one "who is at the right hand of God, who also maketh intercession for us," instead of finding at the throne of grace "One who was in all points tempted like as we are," "a merciful and faithful highpriest," this version of the faith missed the true synthesis of apostolic Christianity by failing to do

98

justice to the divine humanity of the Lord as both redeemer and judge.

viii

From the very outset part of the significance of Jesus was that he could be and was regarded as a pattern for his followers. This was entirely consonant with reverence for him as the object of faith and worship or as authoritative for experience. It is an error in perspective to regard the two aspects as mutually exclusive. No one indeed who wrote an account of Jesus or who referred to his human character ever dreamed of portraying him as ideal man or as a moral pattern and no more for his worshippers. Yet two writings which present Jesus as the Son of God in preeminent glory bear distinct witness to the truth that his life on earth was in some sense and to some degree an example for the religious behavior of Christians. He had left a rule to be obeyed and a line to be followed.

The first three Gospels do not, in so many words, represent Jesus calling for personal imitation of himself. They prefer to express this truth in terms of loyalty. His inner circle of adherents are summoned to follow him, not to copy him, though the one means the other. But in John's Gospel, which stresses union with Christ as the vital center of the Christian life, there is an explicit recognition of the Lord's life on earth as an example of humble service. When Jesus at the Last Supper washed the feet of the disciples, he explained, "I have given you an example that you should do as I have done to you." Later in the evening he added, "I give you a new commandment, to love one another; as I have loved you, so you are to love one another." The spirit which is to rule the fellowship or household of the faith is inspired by his example of humble, self-sacrificing devotion.

Again, the writer of Hebrews, after portraying the unique sacrifice of the Lord for sin and his supreme position in heaven, does not hesitate to present Jesus as the pattern no less than the power of faith. He summons Christians to fix their eyes upon Jesus as "the pioneer and perfection of faith," if they would be true to the heroic course. For this writer the Jesus who alone mediates our approach to God by his perfect sacrifice, is also the supreme exemplar of confidence in God. Bear him in mind, "the Jesus who steadily endured the cross and is now seated at the right hand of the throne of God, so as to keep your own hearts from fainting and falling." What underlies the plea is not that the Lord inspires faith, but that he gives a lead to faith for those who are trying to believe in God and to be loyal, a lead such as no other can, since he himself is the great Believer who exhibited faith from beginning to end in his own career of obedience and service upon earth. The great High Priest was no mere functionary; he was a real person. He had given a living example of human faithfulness to God when he met and mastered such trials as shame and pain.

100

The latter passage marks a common line of interest in the imitation of the Lord. At the very outset Paul had praised some of his Macedonian converts for copying the Lord by their steady endurance and inward joy under persecution. "You started to copy us and the Lord, welcoming the word, though it brought you heavy trouble, with a joy inspired by the holy Spirit." There were touching instances of individuals even imitating some detail in the Passion narrative of Jesus. Thus, when a persecution had broken out against the local church at Smyrna, instigated by some malignant Jews, as had been the case at Thessalonica a century earlier, old Bishop Polycarp surprised his people. A few enthusiasts insisted that the faithful should come forward voluntarily and confess their faith, instead of waiting to be arrested. This was not always attended with the happiest results, for at least one of these ardent souls recanted at the sight of the torture inflicted on his fellows. But the wise old bishop remained where he was. Instead of courting martyrdom, we read, "he waited to be betrayed, as the Lord had waited."[21]

More frequently, however, the example of Jesus was taken in a general sense. He had not only shown the line of God in human life; he was the Leader of the faithful along that line. They copied or followed him in a wider sense than the primitive disciples had done. This was illustrated when a monk of the fifteenth century, belonging to an Augustinian order in

---

[21] 1 Thessalonians i. 6; *Martyrdom of Polycarp* i.

the Netherlands, wrote a devotional book in four parts, the first of which has given its conventional title to the treatise. Indeed it is only the first chapter of the first part which is called *The Imitation of Christ,* and it begins by citing a sentence from the Fourth Gospel: "He that followeth me shall not walk in darkness." The following of Christ is no outward imitation of the language or habits of Jesus, but a life of devout obedience to his words and Spirit. The Cross becomes the symbol not of redeeming power so much as of that renunciation of the world which marks the true Christian. It is the Christian taking up his cross daily and following the Lord, that à Kempis describes, with a spiritual power which often rises above his monastic limitations. Hardly a reference to Mark's Gospel is to be found in these pages. There is far less interest in the earthly life of Jesus than is to be felt in the sermons preached by à Kempis on the life and Passion of the Lord. When Jowett of Balliol read the book, he asked himself if it was possible "to feel a personal attachment to Christ such as that prescribed by Thomas à Kempis? I think that it is impossible and contrary to human nature that we should be able to concentrate our thoughts on a person scarcely known to us, who lived eighteen hundred years ago." Jowett lived at a period when the methods and results of historical criticism appeared to be evaporating nearly all the data about Jesus on earth. He clung wistfully to the idea that one might satisfy the longing for truth and goodness by speaking of it con-

JESUS CHRIST THE SAME

veniently as the life of Christ, making the gospel stories symbolical expressions of a Christian ideal. Yet à Kempis never asked his readers to concentrate upon a distant Jesus of history. His special type of devotion implied a living Lord who had once lived on earth, and who was living in the fellowship of the Church.

When the early Church repeated to the pagan world some words of Jesus about the call to "be perfect as the heavenly Father is perfect," as kind and generous even to the undeserving as the Father is, this saying, with the thought but not the word of imitation, must have wakened in the minds of many an echo of similar teaching by the better spirits of Roman Stoicism. Had not the emperor Aurelius insisted that "the gods do not want to be flattered but to be imitated" by rational creatures? Had not Epictetus taught that "anyone who is to please and obey the gods must endeavor as far as possible to make himself like them" in beneficence and faithfulness? Had not Seneca, even more aptly, told his readers, "If you are imitating the gods, bestow your benefits even on the undeserving, for the sun rises even on scoundrels, and the seas lie open even to pirates"?[22] Jewish-born members of the Church had a still closer approach to this truth than was possible in the cosmic theism of the outside world, for to them the imitation of God meant honor paid to the Deity by reproducing such qualities as beneficence, mercy, and loving-kindness in a life devoted to his service. Man, it was held,

[22] Marcus Aurelius x. 8; Epictetus ii. 14. 13; *De Beneficiis* iv. 26. 1.

had been created in the divine likeness, and therefore
ought to be morally like his Maker, embodying his
kindly attributes. Indeed for some of the later rabbis,
holiness amounted practically to the imitation of God
in this sense.[23] There was a place for this imitation
of God in Christian ethic. The divine character was
put forward as a model for active, affectionate behavior
in the Church, though, as it happens, the one primitive
Christian echo of the command to "be holy as God is
holy" occurs in a wider context than that of opposition
to self-sacrifice and of unbrotherliness.[24] On the whole,
however, the imitation of God soon included Jesus
Christ. When Tertullian in his great tract on Patience
(ii, iii) set himself to prove that patience was in the
nature of God, he began by pointing to the Divine
Providence which continued to shower the benefits of
nature on undeserving sinners, as well as on saints;
but he proceeded to exhibit the supreme proof of it in
the human life of the divine Lord, which is held up
as our example. This correlation had already been
made in the New Testament, though not in connection
with nature. No sooner had the Church recognized
the character of the Father as forgiving and loving,
than it became natural to say of the Son, "be kind to
each other, be tenderhearted, be generous to each other

---

[23] See Schechter's *Some Aspects of Rabbinic Judaism* (chap. xiii), and
Abrahams' *Studies in Pharisaism and the Gospels,* 2d series (pp. 138-182).

[24] 1 Peter i. 14f.: "Instead of molding yourselves to passions that once
ruled you in the days of your ignorance, as He who called you is holy, so
you must be holy too in all your conduct—for it is written, You shall be
holy because I am holy."

104

as God has been generous to you in Christ. Copy God, then, as his beloved children, and lead lives of love, just as Christ loved you and gave himself up for you."

Nowadays the usage has come to be different. The divine qualities of tenderness and pity are associated as a rule with what is Christlike. "Godlike" denotes moral or mental excellence, and is generally associated with strong, upright character of exceptionally high rank; we are more apt to think of Christlike forgiveness and of Godlike dignity or power. Shakespeare and Coleridge have taught us to talk about godlike reason, whereas in the first early centuries of the Faith "godlike" would have covered not merely the faculty of reason but more often the life that gives freely and forgives, as for example in the Epistle to Diognetus (x. 2-6), where God's love is shown in creating mankind, "to whom he gave reason and intelligence, whom he made in his own likeness, to whom he sent his only-begotten Son. . . . By loving him you will become an imitator of his goodness. And do not wonder how a man can be an imitator of God. By God's will he can. For happiness does not mean domineering over one's neighbors, nor longing to have more than poorer men, nor growing rich and using force against weaker people; no one can imitate God in these ways, for they are far from his majesty. But whoever lifts the burden of his neighbor, whoever ministers to the needy, he it is who imitates God."

When Paul appeals to this example of Christ, he is

thinking of the whole life of the Lord in its spirit rather than in detail, of one who "born in human guise and appearing in human form, humbly stooped in his obedience even to die and to die upon the cross." This obedience includes his ministry on earth. The apostle's recollection of his "gentleness and consideration" is inspired by some knowledge of the actual life of Jesus. "He must have known something of Jesus' efforts to win the souls of men, of his deeds of mercy to the suffering, and of his consoling and strengthening intercourse with the lost,"[25] particularly of his consideration for human weaknesses, his sympathy with the outcast, and his self-renouncing love. This is the special feature to which Paul recurs, as in pleading with some Roman Christians to take a higher way than that of selfish individualism and disregard for other people. "We are not to please ourselves; each of us must please his neighbor, doing him good by building up his faith," however hard it may be to stand the petty scruples of those who make things difficult for themselves and their fellow Christians by narrow ideas of religion. No Christian has a right to stand stiffly on his rights, or to brush aside conscientious objections felt by unintelligent members of the society. Why? For this clinching reason: "Christ certainly did not please himself." Paul's hearers and readers knew what he meant. It was familiar to them in their simple knowledge of Jesus

---

[25] Johannes Weiss, *Paul and Jesus* (pp. 93f.) ; so in his *History of Primitive Christianity* (pp. 452f.).

among men. Indeed this was the quality of his character which the apostle commonly recalled in his admonitions. The climax of Christ's thoughtfulness for others was the sacrifice upon the cross, but the allusions[26] are not to be confined to this, much less to be explained as inferences from the descent of a heavenly Lord to this world of men. It was not conceptions like those of the Son of man or messiah or Wisdom which prompted Paul to speak of "the Son of God who loved me and gave himself up for me." Rather it was the impression of the Lord's actual life that put new color into such cloudy notions and made them rich with new significance for the Church. Paul was not merely drawing on messianic or other myths of a divine agent swooping or stooping to earth. Such ethical qualities are absent from the dreams of earlier and contemporary religious fancy. It required a definite personality to account for Paul's emphasis on humble self-sacrifice in his Christ.

As crucifixion was the capital punishment for slaves, it was specially appropriate for Peter or a later writer to encourage Christian slaves by recalling them to the example of Christ in his passion, who endured injustice and pain without retaliating. "To this you have been called, because Christ also suffered for you, leaving you an example, to follow in his footsteps." Without forgetting that these sufferings were redemptive, Peter holds them up as a pattern of humble, patient submis-

---

[26] Philippians ii. 7f.; 2 Corinthians x. 1; Romans xv. 1-3.

107

siveness to a class of society which was considered as a rule to be beneath the level of ordinary ethics. So, in a tract belonging to the Johannine circle, the example of the Lord is put forward, though not in a passive connection. The redeeming Christ is not only the indwelling Christ but a Christ to be imitated by Christians, that is, a Christ with demands and commands. "Anyone who says, I abide in him," claiming this mystical union, "ought himself to be living as he lived." He who is "the propitiation for our sins" is also to be followed in the moral obedience of life to the new commandment of love. The appeal of the writer implies, if not personal reminiscences, at any rate reminiscences of a person. The human character of the Lord in our human scene is the presupposition of the argument.[27] Christianity has no place for any spiritual mysticism which dispenses with the historical Christ and his new commandment of love.

A religious genius like Luther occasionally took exception to the cult of imitating Jesus, as he found it in some medieval mystics. Their language sounded to him as though Christianity were being presented as a human effort to reproduce the divine life, instead of an humble acceptance of God's power and promise by faith. "Imitation does not make people sons of God," he wrote;[28] "it is sonship that makes them imitators

---

[27] 1 Peter ii. 21f.; 1 John ii. 6.
[28] Commenting on Galatians iii. 14. His reasons for suspecting this specious pseudo-imitation are noted by Karl Holl in *Gesammelte Aufsätze zur Kirchengeschichte* i., pp. 308, 433f.

of God." Luther had read the New Testament too well to forget that Christianity for every man is a new creation, not the result of setting up Christ as a model to be carefully copied in externals. This danger was not on the horizon of the primitive Church. Yet one significant fact points to a similar sensitiveness. The original term "disciples" had gone beyond Judaism by including women, but it was soon dropped. It was felt that this metaphor might misrepresent the faith to the Greek and Roman world, as though Christianity were another philosophical sect which adhered to the axioms of its dead leader. Other equivalents, like "followers" or "servants," were used to denote the relation of Christians to their Master and Lord. They had never indeed thought of themselves as disciples in the Greek sense of the term. The very idea of disciples implied that pupils must at all costs abide by the instructions of their teacher. But the distinctive thing about Christianity was that this obedience to the Master had been inspired by a reverence which deepened into worship. Consequently the metaphor was not merely susceptible of misinterpretation; it ceased to be adequate. Eventually the term was reserved for brave confessors or martyrs, as a special term of honor. Such heroic spirits alone were believed to have imitated their Lord in the supreme sacrifice.[29] There was some loss here, for the

---

[29] "We rightly love the martyrs as disciples and imitators of the Lord, for their unsurpassed devotion of heart to their King and Master" (Martyrdom of Polycarp xvii).

popular appreciation of the vital connection between the character and the teaching of Jesus often suffered, just as in modern days the reaction toward a study of his ethical principles has too often been divorced from any serious conviction of his person. But no changes of language affect the fact that Christians are called to live as Jesus taught, because he lived as he taught, and once lived a truly human life. "Amid all the sins and failings, amid all the priestcraft and persecution and fanaticism that have defaced the Church, it has preserved, in the character and example of its Founder, an enduring principle of regeneration."[30] Whatever the Church may think and hold about regeneration, this verdict of the agnostic historian is justified. The example of Jesus Christ has repeatedly stirred and shamed his followers with an appeal which is not confined to them. But for them it ought to be of vital moment, since what God requires from us is best understood by what he has done for us. His standard for human life is revealed through the life and character of Jesus his Son, with its embodiment of self-sacrificial love as the supreme expression of what is wonderful in the divine kindness. The example lies in the character, which is so far above men and yet within reach of all. The imitation of God is not response to this precept or that, so much as to the personal life which reaches the heart and conscience through any demands, in order to be reproduced by those who see God in Jesus, as he is not

---

[30]Lecky, *History of European Morals* (chap. iv).

110

seen elsewhere. At the same time it is the response of obedience to authority. To copy the Lord is, in its essence for Christians, to follow him in his divine humanity. Any adoration or any admiration which fails to include this quality is out of line with the conception of his example in historical Christianity. Jesus showed man what he might become, by revealing God as he is; he did so by becoming man himself. Not that he was the supreme illustration of what man may be or do. He was more than an example. Christ is Christ, and we are Christians. But, if the revelation is to be realized, it must include some reproduction of the divine character which he embodied.

ix

To the student of history, who knows the religious craving for mythology, evident both within and outside the non-canonical Gospels, it is a constant wonder how the personality of Jesus was explained, not eclipsed or distorted, by the adoring reverence of the primitive churches for his divine humanity. Too often the opposite has been the case in later Christendom. But there has been an irrepressible instinct to distrust any depreciation of what he was and said and did. However exalted truth may be, as Sainte-Beuve observed in another connection, it requires to be made man in order to touch men.[31] In Jesus Christ, as the Church

---

[31] In *Port-Royale* (ii. 170) : La vérité, si haute qu'elle soit, a besoin de se faire homme pour toucher les hommes.

knows him, we touch God's "presence and his very self and essence all divine." In and through history, by something that happened in a definite time and a definite place, faith touches One who is the center of life. When this conviction is infringed by any theological or critical attitude toward the Gospels in which it is recorded, there is a reaction on the part of those who are not afraid to hold that all they know of the Absolute is bound up with the story of One who once lived a life of real limitations in this world. This was what prompted Santa Teresa to enter a passionate protest against some highflying mystics of the contemplative kind in her community who sought to discourage anything like meditation upon the sacred humanity of the Lord Jesus. "Nothing," she declared, "nothing will induce me to admit that it is best to exercise oneself in what concerns the divinity and to avoid what is bodily"[32] in him, as though one could get past Jesus in reaching heights of rapture and contemplation. Half a century earlier, Martin Luther had been faced by the same danger in another quarter, as scholastic teachers of his day seemed to be neglecting Jesus in their dogmatic speculations on the being and substance of Christ in the Godhead. It is not so, Luther pled, that Christ can be learned. Luther was too good a scholar to depreciate creeds and dogma, but he insisted that an educational course which started with such ab-

[32] *The Interior Castle* (vi. 6-9).

stract problems blurred any natural and direct realization of the Lord, when it presupposed that the mystery of his being had to be approached through technical formulas of metaphysics, instead of beginning with the revelation of God in the gospel records. As he once put it in a Trinity sermon,[33] "We cannot have any surer basis for the divinity of Christ than as we enwrap and enclose our hearts in what scripture says; for scripture raises us gently and gradually, bringing us to Christ first as man, then as Lord over all creatures, and then as God. This is how I reach the end and know God. But philosophers and sages of the world begin at the top and so become fools." What Teresa and Luther rejected still makes its appeal in other forms. Thus, it will never do to depreciate the human personality of Jesus on earth, on the ground that this belongs merely to the domain of historical perception, whereas divine revelation belongs to a higher category; the primitive Church did not think of the Lord's humanity as an incognito of his divine nature. It is equally irrelevant, from another angle, to argue that the one thing important to the first believers must have been, not the character of Jesus Christ but what God had done through him, as though his character could be separated from his commission. This is to diminish the historical medium of revelation, even when it is argued in terms of an evangelical interpretation.

[33] Erlangen edition (xii. 381).

X

The considerations which have been presented will explain why it is at this point that historic Christianity diverges not only from the ultra-mystical hypothesis that past history means little or nothing to the immediate consciousness of God in the living present, but from an idealistic philosophy like that of Croce, who holds that the past cannot be said to exist at all except in the active thought and historical imagination of today, as the historian feels the aims and actions of remote ages vibrating within his trained consciousness. This is far from the Christian position. It is an axiom of the faith that our recollection of the past is due to a sense of its lasting and effective value for ourselves. To Croce any such pragmatic aim is naturally a fruitful source of error. But when we "do this in remembrance of" the Lord, or remember his sayings, it is not, it never has been, from a disinterested desire to study the far past of our religion; we do so in order to renew faith and obedience. We seek to reassure ourselves that it is true, for practical reasons. Furthermore, we believe that there is a reading of that past which is more true than any other, certainly more true than any purely objective interpretation, a reading which is bound up with the supreme and creative life of Jesus the Christ of God. It is only in connection with personalities that we can properly speak of a living past. All religion moves in the sphere of worlds not yet realized. Chris-

114

tians believe in a purpose of God that is to be fully
realized, since it has already entered into human experience and history with the promise of ultimate
achievement. Those who first enjoyed the revelation
of Christ knew that they were tasting "the powers of
the world to come." It might even be said that they
read the history of the past in the light of the future,
since their assurance of the end threw light back upon
the present; the meaning of today lay in what had happened yesterday at the incarnation, and in what the
incarnation involved for days to come. It was in such
a perspective that they viewed history. Thus and thus
only they were conscious of knowing God as living and
loving. For whatever the incarnation means, "it means
at least this, that in the conditions of human life we
have access, as nowhere else, to the inmost nature of
the divine. 'God manifest in the flesh' is a more
profound, philosophical truth than the loftiest flights
of speculation that outsoars all predicates and for the
greater glory of God declares him unknowable."[34]
Which in turn implies that the incarnation means not
only God meeting us in Christ, but also Christ meeting
us in his followers. The latter truth is far more vital
than is commonly recognized. Nowhere is the danger
of the half-truth more insidious than here. "Who is
he that overcometh the world but he that believeth
that Jesus is the Son of God?" The ultimate triumph
belongs to this worship alone, not to any cult of a semi-

---

[34] A. S. Pringle-Pattison in *The Idea of God*, p. 157.

human Christ or a semi-divine Jesus, much less to any idolatry of the human self. True, but the same writer is careful to insist that this is bound up with devotion to the ends and interests of God in one's fellow creatures; God's command is, "that we should believe in the name of his Son Jesus Christ and love one another as he has commanded us to do." It is to isolate and narrow the truth of the divine humanity in Jesus if we try to hold it without a full recognition of how it is to be verified in the practice of brotherly love. "Inasmuch as ye have done it to one of the least of these my brethren, ye have done it to me." Jesus had in his life and teaching pressed this on the conscience of his followers, that the cold heart as well as the proud mind darkens man's vision of God. He identified himself with his community. His real presence was to be experienced in their service. He could speak more explicitly of this aspect than even of his own divinity. Yet there is a constant tension between the two poles. Some indeed who cannot as yet go further than to call Jesus Leader, often exhibit a loyalty to the test and task of brotherly love as love to him, which is a reproach and challenge to those who call him Lord. But the Church is vital as it recognizes the incarnation in both revelations, of God and of man, through the Jesus of history. It is when one side or the other is permitted to absorb the mind, that the conviction of the Lord's divine humanity becomes inadequate.

116

Part Three

Not long ago a jesuit in paris told his audience, "Suppose that Jesus came holding in one hand the eucharist and in the other the Gospels, and said to you, 'I give you the choice, My person in the Host, or the story of my life in the Book; which do you prefer?' At the risk of startling you, I say that I would answer, 'Lord, since I cannot have both treasures at once, keep your eucharist and give me the Gospels.' "[1] Of course he at once added that the eucharist, with its content of Jesus in flesh and in Spirit, depended upon the Book, and that God had not chosen to give us the one without the other. This answer points to a true perspective for understanding the supreme significance of the New Testament for the Church, as a book of worship for the fellowship, which insures access to the living God. The historian knows that worship or the liturgy has from the first been as vital a factor in Christianity as it had been in the heritage of Israel. Such worship is inspired by definite historical events; now as always it is in using the New Testament to understand them, by frequenting the sacraments which belong to them, by seeking and finding the living Word in the written Word, that Christians enjoy and verify the truth that

---

[1] H. Pinard de la Boullaye, in *Jésus et l'Histoire*, pp. 180f.

117

God through Jesus Christ is dealing with them and revealed afresh to their need of him.

i

This does not amount to pious associations and sentimental memories clinging to some half-beliefs about a book whose historical records are neither very clear nor certain. It is the sure faith of vital Christianity to recognize that, as early as we can identify the Christian religion, it was a religion about Jesus Christ. The recognition is not invariably based upon the arguments once adduced in support of it. Today our background of thinking is not that of the first or of any later century. But the foreground remains the same. "Men may preach Christ though they do not name Christ in every sentence and period of words." One is reminded of Whichcote's aphorism in connection with two apostolic speeches where the name of Jesus is not mentioned, and yet where his significance is uppermost. Both Stephen and Paul were interrupted as they reached the critical point, Stephen by Jews at Jerusalem who passionately resented his assertion that "the Just One" had denied the finality of temple-worship, Paul by a group of the intelligentsia at Athens who were willing to listen to an introductory talk on the philosophy of religion in history but had no patience with a strolling evangelist who insisted that God had "fixed a day for judging the world by a man destined for this, and had given proof of this by raising him from the dead."

118

Neither Stephen nor Paul needed as yet to mention the actual person to whom they referred. Their hearers did not require to be told his name; they broke up the meeting in each case because they knew that what was now to be said about the risen Jesus would be an insult to their pride and prejudice of faith, in the one case, and of intelligence in the other. Everybody knew that when the propaganda of this new faith was active, the one name on the lips of the leaders was sooner or later that of Jesus.

Paul's Athenian speech provides an instance of Jesus being supplied. Instead of "a man destined for this," codex Bezae and the old Latin version of Irenaeus read "a [or, the] man Jesus." This practice was sometimes followed, when the usual text read simply "he" (as in Matthew iv. 23; John xxi. 17; Galatians vi. 12; 2 Corinthians iv. 6; Romans viii. 34). There are more than twenty cases of it in Mark's Gospel, where "Jesus" occurs much more seldom in narrative than in Matthew, the reason perhaps[2] being that, as the evangelist is drawing on reminiscences of Peter, Peter would frequently be content to say "he," since there could be no question who was meant. In the special source of Luke's Gospel, the name of "Jesus" is now and then inserted in the text instead of "Lord," by several texts and versions, particularly by the Sinaitic Syriac (e. g., at vii. 13, 18, x. 1, 39, 41, xiii. 15, xviii. 6, and even xix. 8, all narratives), as though many Christians loved to

[2] C. H. Turner, *Journal of Theological Studies,* xxvi, p. 226.

have the personal name of Jesus in the record. Neither here nor elsewhere is there any dogmatic interest.[3] "Lord" is what Luke found in his source. For him "the Christ" means messiah, and he avoids phrases like "Jesus Christ" or even "Jesus who is called Christ." But one significant difference of reading occurs in the pastoral letter of Saint Judas, who reminds his readers how "the Lord saved the people out of the land of Egypt." Some texts made it perfectly clear by reading "God." But, as a few early texts and a number of versions (the Latin, Egyptian, and Ethiopic) show, there was a rival reading, "Jesus," although it is fair to add that several Christian thinkers, like Lactantius and Jerome, understood this to mean Joshua (which in Greek is the same as Jesus); Joshua was supposed by them to personify Jesus, for few Christians appear to have agreed with the author of Barnabas,[4] that the Church had the incarnate Jesus, while Israel had no more than a Jesus or Joshua who merely opened up a material land of promise. If Saint Judas wrote "Jesus" in the sense of Lord, it would be exceptional, for both Paul and the writer of Hebrews use "Christ" in referring to the Son of God prior to the incarnation.

There are comparatively few traces of "Jesus" being omitted from the text; the evidence in such cases is weak, for "Jesus" was not in the original text of pas-

---

[3] Vincent Taylor, *Behind the Third Gospel*, pp. 265, 266.
[4] vi. 9. "Put your hope in the Jesus who is to be manifested to you in the flesh," opening up the new creation and spiritual sphere of Christ.

sages like 2 Corinthians iv. 6; Romans viii. 34; and Galatians vi. 12. The tendency was rather to amplify "Jesus" by adding "Lord" or "Christ." Sometimes the full phrase is authentic, as in Acts xx. 21 and xxviii. 31 or 1 Corinthians vi. 11, but scribes often wrote "Christ" or "Lord" to supplement the name of Jesus. On the other hand, as Paul uses "Christ" frequently in the sense of deliverer or Saviour, the wide and early Western evidence for omitting "Jesus" in Galatians v. 24 is unconvincing, even although "those who belong to Christ Jesus" is unusual. Similarly "the marks of the Lord Jesus" (in Galatians vi. 17) is more likely to be right than "the marks of the Lord Jesus Christ," if any addition to Jesus is needed at all.

It has become convenient to speak about the Jesus of history and the spiritual Christ, or about the historical Jesus and the Christ of faith. But these modern phrases do not exactly correspond to the facts. In the primitive strata of tradition, "Jesus" is naturally the name used for our Lord on earth; in order to distinguish him from others of the same name, he is sometimes called Jesus of Nazareth. Jesus was indeed his personal name. But on the lips of early Christians it was not limited to his earthly ministry. When Christians spoke of what we call the spiritual Christ, they sometimes said "Jesus" quite freely, without adding any divine title. The author of Hebrews does this. So does Saint Paul. So does the prophet John in the book of Revelation. If we are to judge from the evidence of the Acts of the

Apostles, which probably reflects, not any usage of Luke himself but the actual custom of primitive Palestinian Christians, men like Stephen and the good Ananias employed the term "Jesus" for the living Lord in heaven. Three times over Luke makes Paul tell the story of his conversion; the accounts are not verbally identical (which throws a sidelight on the comparative freedom with which a story could be told in Christian literature), but one feature in all three versions of the incident is the same; the heavenly Lord declares, "I am Jesus, and you are persecuting me." It is not merely that Jesus identifies himself with his followers and worshippers at Damascus and elsewhere, but the risen Lord is Jesus, the historical Jesus and more. The name is used of him as risen and reigning.

Paul preached Jesus. We know what that meant to him. Nowadays to preach Jesus may mean anything or nothing, that is, little or nothing that answers to the apostolic gospel. But when the apostle preached Jesus, as at Athens, it was Jesus and the resurrection, a religion of new vistas for thought and experience. And he taught this message in no stereotyped fashion. There are distinct differences of emphasis between the conception of Jesus in the letters to Thessalonica, for example, and the letters to the Colossians and Philippians; in the later letters the pre-eminence of the Lord is outlined, not only with regard to salvation but also to creation and the cosmos, as Paul now traces a purpose of the God in the universe which is revealed through

122

Christ to the Church, and is to be realized through the Church. How this conception of Christ as active in creation came to be developed is a difficult problem. It rose not from anything that Jesus himself had said, but from a consciousness in the Church that this was implicit in his relation to God.[5] It may well have been present to Paul's mind before he wrote his later letters, for all his letters were written in the late afternoon of his life, and he developed truth as it was needed in view of special exigencies in the churches. But, however we explain the problem, it is the same Jesus and no other. What underlies the cosmic conception of Christ in Paul and in the Fourth Gospel is faith in what Jesus had been and in what he was to the world of God. Christianity as the religion of the incarnation includes a recognition of the worth attaching to nature as well as to history.

Sometimes Jesus is called Lord in the sense of "sir," a courtesy title, as by the father of the epileptic boy or the Syro-Phoenician woman, but more often by his disciples and the outside public in the sense of an authority on things divine. Even when he is called teacher or rabbi, the general sense of chief or something like this must be assumed. Thus Matthew occasionally turns the term into Lord, and five times over Luke makes it clearer to his non-Jewish readers by employing a special Greek word (*epistatês*) for Master,

---

[5] This is admirably argued in Professor J. M. Creed's Hulsean lectures on *The Divinity of Jesus Christ*, pp. 137-143.

which denoted leader or one to be obeyed. Indeed "teacher" itself ought to be rendered "Master"; the English word has a conveniently double significance which answers exactly to the range of the term as applied to Jesus. He is not always addressed as a mere teacher or rabbi. Martha's remark to her sister, "The teacher has come," is not fully rendered even by printing "teacher" with a capital T. "The Master" is more adequate, for Jesus here is the man of God with power. Jerome was correct in explaining "rabbi" as "master" or "my master." The substitution of Lord or Master for Mark's rabbi or teacher, is not necessarily a proof of later interpretation by evangelists who read more into the term than it originally possessed in the tradition; often the change is due to a correct perception that the term held more authority than the other rendering suggested. Thus, when the blind beggar in Mark's story cried, "Rabboni, I would regain my sight," Matthew and Luke rightly rendered "rabboni" by "Lord," for again it was not the teacher but the religious healer, the Son of David, who was invoked as Lord. The truth is, Lord, teacher, rabbi, or rabboni, reflect a common attitude toward Jesus which ranges from deep respect to reverence.

Some churches were so sensitive to the recognition of their Lord as the one and only Jesus that they altered a passage in the Passion story, as Matthew[6] told it. When the Jerusalemite Jews gathered before Pilate,

---

[6] xxvii. 16, 17.

124

he said to them, "Whom do you want released? Jesus Bar-Abbas or Jesus the so-called Christ?" referring to a notorious prisoner of the day. Nearly all the later church texts deprived the criminal of his first name, not because they wanted to bring Matthew's text into line with the other Gospels but because they were shocked at the idea of this rascal sharing the name of their Lord. Such was their intense reverence for the name of Jesus that they disliked to think of Bar-Abbas having been his namesake. In recent days this feeling was strongly voiced by the textual critic, Dean Burgon.[7] But it was urged by Origen in the second century, though he knew that many ancient copies of the Gospel contained "Jesus Bar-Abbas," and admitted that a name might be borne by bad men no less than by good, as in the case of Judas or Ananias. When Professor Burkitt[8] upheld the authenticity of the tradition, the main textual evidence available was from Syria, particularly from the Sinaitic and Syriac versions. Now it has the support of the Koridethi text, so that the reading is rooted also in this important Caesarean form of the early evangelic text. There is no satisfactory explanation of how or why such a reading could have been inserted. On the other hand it is obvious why it would be cut out by Christians, for whom there was but one Jesus.

---

[7] *Causes of Corruption in the Traditional Text,* pp. 53-55.
[8] *Evangelion da-Mepharreshe* ii. pp. 277f.; so Deissmann in *Mysterium Christi,* pp. 19-21.

Once indeed in the New Testament "another Jesus" is mentioned, but this very allusion corroborates the fact that there was only one for Christendom. It occurs in a passionate passage of self-defense,[9] dictated by Paul to the church at Corinth. The paragraph is far from easy, but the argument seems to be this: he is reproaching some local Christians for having listened to evangelists who had discredited his authority in order to discredit the truth of his gospel. Surely, the apostle writes, with indignant irony, surely they might put up with him and give him a hearing, after he had initiated them into the faith, as they had put up with vagrant missioners who had made their appearance at Corinth with a new theology. "You put up with it all right," he sarcastically observes, "when some interloper preaches another Jesus (not the Jesus I preached)." He is taunting them with tolerating some person or party who brought new opinions about Jesus, probably Palestinian Christians of the narrower type who heralded a "Christ according to the flesh," a Jesus who was no more than a messianic figure, and whose mission was to fulfill the nationalist hopes of Jews on the old lines of the Law. To Paul this was a misrepresentation of the spiritual Jesus Christ. He had told the Galatian Christians that if they listened to any such propaganda, they were in danger of going over to another gospel altogether, or rather to a distorted form of the gospel of

[9] 2 Corinthians xi. 1-13.

Jesus Christ. Here he alludes to the same subject in passing, as it affects his own credentials. These missioners had assured the Corinthian church that they, in the wake of the original apostles, knew much more about the real Jesus than this upstart Paul. He retaliates that theirs is a spurious gospel, a deflection from the "single devotion to Christ" which was the heart of his message. To him this reading of the Lord's character is as defective as George Moore's "pale socialist of Galilee" is to anyone inside the Church. Without entering into the merits of the question, he sarcastically asks if the Corinthians will not give him the same consideration as they extended to his critics, these spurious apostles who masquerade as apostles of Christ. Do put up with me for a moment, as I defend myself against the charge of having actually given you the gospel for nothing, free of charge! "You put up with it all right when you get a wrong gospel. You put up with it all right when some interloper preaches a second Jesus (not the Jesus I preach), or when you are treated to a Spirit different from the Spirit you once received, and to a different gospel from what I gave you."

So the appeal runs. Paul is genuinely concerned. He is afraid of the local church allowing itself to be seduced from single-minded devotion to Christ by such cunning, devilish insinuations as are being circulated at Corinth. But many in the early Church, who read

127

this passage, were reluctant to believe that the situation was anything except imaginary. How could Paul be alluding to a real event? There was only one Jesus. So, often altering the text a little, they read it as if it meant a hypothetical case, as though he wrote, "If such a thing were to occur, if actually anyone did preach another Jesus, you might well bear with him." Why? Because, Paul must have meant, "you already know the full truth about Jesus from me. You could afford to put up with any errorists, even if they were to proclaim such an absurdity as another Jesus." Our English versions, following the Vulgate, usually take the paragraph in this sense. But it is a prosaic and forced interpretation, missing the sharp irony with which the passage is charged. What Paul has in mind, as he dictates this sarcastic sentence, is an actual misrepresentation of Jesus which was being spread at Corinth. He will not allow for a moment that he is less interested in Jesus or less acquainted with what Jesus had meant by his life on earth, than these emissaries from Jerusalem. The whole passage is significant for the sidelight which it throws, not merely on the threefold synthesis of Jesus, the Spirit, and the gospel, but also on the misplaced concern of later generations to safeguard the identity of Jesus in the apostolic preaching. It was right for them to believe that there could never have been any Jesus except one. It was needless to treat Paul's argument as if it threw any doubt on this, and to alter the text accordingly.

128

ii

Yet the followers of Jesus were not called after him. Eventually they came to adopt a nickname coined for them by some clever pagans, who wanted a word to label what was neither a Jewish nor an ethnic movement. The witty Antiochenes dubbed members of this cult "Christians." Needless to say, this did not mean messianists. It was a term for the household or party who belonged to Christ. For by this time "Christ" was beginning to be used as a proper name for Jesus. Once or twice the apostle Paul employs the word in the general sense of messiah, but as a rule it is otherwise. One of the remarkable things in the vocabulary of early Christendom is that the company of Jesus appears to have felt that "the Christ," this title of honor and hope, could only be borne by Jesus their Lord. In arguing with Jews they might still speak of "the Christ," as he himself had done upon occasion, but to themselves he was Jesus the Christ, or simply Jesus Christ. Such a shift of language implies that the ambiguous category of messianism was being superseded by the conviction that he shared the divine authority and nature; he was Son of the Father, at God's right hand, and also within the hearts of his worshipping community. For this unique relationship traditional terms now assumed fresh meaning. It was no longer enough to say that Jesus was the Christ, the divinely consecrated messiah or Son of David, true though that might be. Even prior to Paul, Jesus was called Christ, and "Lord" became only a more intelligible and less provincial title for what his mission involved. As Peter once told a Jerusalem crowd, "God has made him both Lord and Christ, this Jesus whom you crucified." But soon "Christ" passed into a personal name, as an equivalent for Jesus.

Twice only is the term put into the lips of Jesus as a self-designation; for "What think you of Christ?" is a question put to the Pharisees about the meaning of "the Christ" or messiah in their religious tradition. One of these passages[10] belongs to a warning against self-importance, based on deference such as scribes and Pharisees coveted and expected from the people. "They like to be called rabbi by men.

> But you are not to be called rabbi,
>   for One is your teacher, and you are all brothers;
> you are not to call anyone 'father' on earth,
>   for One is your heavenly Father."

Then the editor adds, as a variation on the former allusion,

> "Nor must you be called leaders,
>   for One is your leader, even the Christ."

"Leader" here signifies "master," one who gives authoritative directions for life, like a rabbi. But Jesus insists that the disciples are neither to accept the honorific title of rabbi, nor to give the highly esteemed

---

[10] Matthew xxiii. 8-10.

title of father, as though any follower of the Lord could be an authoritative exponent of God's revelation. "Even the Christ" or "even Christ" is a Christian expansion of the original saying, that in the new community there was to be only one Father and only One with authority to teach his revealed will.

The other passage[11] is of importance for other reasons. It was remembered that in commissioning his disciples for a special mission, he had declared with divine authority:

> "He who receives you receives me,
>   and he who receives me receives him who sent me;
> he who receives a prophet because he is a prophet,
>   will receive a prophet's reward;
> he who receives a good man because he is good,
>   will receive a good man's reward."

Then he added, "And whoever gives one of these little ones even a cup of cold water because he is a disciple, I tell you, he shall not lose his reward," alluding to subordinate or obscure members of the mission. For the first time in the history of religion, apparently, Jesus uses "little ones" to mean disciples of a Cause. Here as elsewhere[12] he declares that the simplest hospitality shown to the rank and file will count before God. "One of these little ones" denotes anyone who may be of no great account in the service, compared with

---

[11] Matthew x. 40-42; Mark ix. 41.
[12] Matthew xxv. 31-40. Echoed in John xiii. 20: "He who receives anyone I send, receives me, and he who receives me, receives him who sent me."

131

the apostles, prophets, and eminent Christians to whom Jesus has just been referring. The least important is invested with divine significance, so that what is done to him is done to his divine commissioner.

Such is the original text and sense of the saying, as transmitted by Matthew. Mark, however, preserves it in a less appropriate context and in a slightly different form: "Whoever gives you a cup of cold water because you belong to Christ, I tell you truly, he shall not miss his reward." Literally it is, "in my name" (i. e., because you bear my name), and this is explained as "because you are Christ's." Elsewhere Mark shows a singular sense of historical fitness in avoiding such a term or personal title as "Christ," just as Luke does in refraining from the use of "Lord" on the lips of the disciples when they address Jesus before the resurrection. If the phrase "you belong to Christ" carries its full sense, it would therefore be an anachronism, an unexampled use of the Pauline phrase in Mark's text. The alternative would be to take it as a rendering of some Aramaic phrase like "you belong to messiah" or "to him whom you now own to be messiah." Probably it is a solitary instance of Mark coloring a saying with the later hue of Christian belief. But in any case the original saying again attests the high consciousness of Jesus, as in the name of God he promises that the slightest charity shown to anyone in his mission, however humble, would be rewarded. So important was the mission, in the sight of God, that any person taking

132

part in it deserved to be honored by men, and no outsider who welcomed even a minor figure or humble
missioner with practical kindness, recognizing his character and vocation, would fail to be honored by God.
Since these agents of the Cause represented Jesus, who
himself represented God, any service done to them was
reckoned by him as done to God.

iii

The pre-eminent position which Jesus was conscious
of holding in the divine purpose of the kingdom, is indicated by his next warning. With a passionate indigna-
tion which is the other side of his care for the humble
and inexperienced, he tells his adherents plainly that
they would be better dead than live to damage the soul
of anyone in the childhood of faith! "Whoever is a
hindrance to one of these little ones who believe, it
were better for him to have a great millstone hung
round his neck and be thrown into the sea." The
"little ones" here mean people still in the infancy of
religious faith, who are easily led astray by stronger
natures or even driven to backsliding by bad example
or by harshness on the part of disciples. Some early
texts and versions added "in me" to "believe," in order
to make sure that it was faith in Jesus. This is the
reading in Matthew's text. In Mark it may be a
secondary and dogmatic expansion. But, even without
it, the sense is the same. What is meant is faith in
Jesus, that is, faith in God as elicited by the mission of

133

Jesus. Here and elsewhere his appeal for loyalty and confidence is more than that of a prophet or sage bringing some new word of God; he is founding a society or group to be the nucleus of the new order of fellowship with God, in which he himself has been destined to command the allegiance of men. When he spoke of faith, it was not faith in general, but faith in himself as God's chosen representative. Faith was response to the revelation with which he was charged. When scholars like Loisy insisted that a phrase like "believe in me" was impossible on the lips of the historical Jesus, Montefiore said all that required to be said: "I cannot but think that in virtue of the authority which, as he believed, had been granted him, and of the office which would shortly be his, Jesus, as the representative of God, might well have used some such phrase, or at any rate given the impression which led up to it."[13]

A sidelight upon the same pre-eminence is thrown by the strange story[14] of how Jesus once rebuked John for having disavowed an exorcist who used the name of Jesus in his work. "John said to him," recalling an incident in the recent mission of the disciples, "Master, we saw a man casting out daemons in your name, and so we stopped him. But Jesus said, Do not stop him" (never check a man like that), "for no one who performs any miracle in my name will be ready to speak

---

[13] *Hibbert Journal*, x., pp. 777-78.
[14] Mark ix. 38-40; Luke ix. 49-50.

evil of me. He who is not against us is for us" (i. e., on our side). The story is true to the traditional antipathy of John to anything like schism, and it happens to be the only incident in the life of Jesus where John intervenes. We can only guess at the attitude of the exorcist toward Jesus. The tale is not concerned with him but with the lesson of toleration read to a sincerely intolerant disciple. While Jesus made devotion to himself binding on all his followers, he refused to excommunicate from his cause anyone who did not belong to his regular group, even if the man independently employed the sacred name to cast out evil spirits from human life. There may be a half-ironical tinge in the closing words, as though Jesus felt that it was something at least to have a man who would not be likely to curse or disavow him; such an evangelist, pronouncing my name for a good end, is a friend and ally, for what he is worth; he may not be going all the way with us yet, but he is on the way.

Those who think it unlikely that exorcism in the name of Jesus was used during his lifetime, prefer to take the story in its present form as a tale of the later Church which was intended to disavow the repudiation of Paul by the narrower disciples at Jerusalem, though they knew how Paul used the name of Jesus effectively. This is as ingenious and convincing as the companion theory that the beloved disciple in the Fourth Gospel is the apostle Paul. Fortunately for this theory, the apostle had happened to speak of the Son of God lov-

135

ing him! In any case it is significant that a similar expression of broad-mindedness once came from Paul himself, when in prison and unable to preach Jesus any longer. Others, he wrote,[15] were doing this in their own way, and, though sometimes it was not his way, after all the main thing was to spread the good news. "My imprisonment has given the majority of the brotherhood greater confidence in the Lord to venture upon speaking the word of God without being afraid. Some of them, it is true, are actually preaching Christ from envy and rivalry, taking the opportunity of my enforced silence to spread their own narrower views and to outdo me in my mission. Others do it from good will, from love to me, but the former proclaim Christ for their own ends, with mixed motives, intending to annoy me as I lie in prison and hear of their fresh activities." "What does it matter?" he adds generously. "Anyhow, for ulterior ends or honestly, Christ is being preached. And over that I rejoice; yes and I will rejoice." Preachers who were more in sympathy with the Jewish Christian propaganda, might rejoice to see their rival prevented from preaching his liberal gospel, but Paul was determined to rejoice in nothing except the fact that Christ was becoming better known in the pagan world. The time was short, too short and serious for anything but devotion to the great Cause and its Lord. The apostle was not prepared to unchurch (as we say) men of other opinions.

---

[15] Philippians i. 14-18.

even although these might be defective or inspired by questionable motives. So long as they pointed people to Christ, that was everything. As Jesus had done, he discourages any repression or condemnation of activities which were charged, however imperfectly, with some genuine interest in the essential power of Jesus himself.

iv

No two products of life in the Church during the first four centuries have been more permanent and influential than the Nicene Creed and the New Testament. Both the Creed and the Canon were called into being by the need for direction in seeing Jesus as the Son of God. But while the former was beat out, as it were, in keen discussions, no formal councils were held to fix the Canon. There was no strong hand of ecclesiastical authority at work. Great differences of opinion prevailed for a while upon its contents, and yet the matter was ultimately settled by general consent of the Eastern and the Western churches. The Epistles of Paul were first collected; then followed the four Gospels, though the reasons for their choice are obscure. What is not obscure is the conscious need for some such action; these writings were chosen to be read in worship, as classical documents of the apostolic faith which centered in the gospel of Jesus Christ. When one realizes the books that were once inside the canon for a while, and the greater number which were excluded, it is remarkable how much corporate wisdom was displayed in forming the collection. Those who believe in the working of the Spirit in the early Church are justified in singling out the formation of the canon as a most significant proof of divine guidance.

Yet this new possession led to difficulties as well as to gains. The sacred Book was the same for all the churches, and carefully prized by most, who were stimulated to study it with loving care. It is a historical illusion, of course, to imagine the Church during the early centuries reading the New Testament and nothing else; the luxuriant growth of religious fiction in the non-canonical Gospels and other popular literature was preparing the Christian mythology which presently gathered round the person of the Lord in more than heretical circles. Still, the New Testament alone was read in the worship of the one God and the one Son of God. The awkward thing was that when the new collection was studied by itself as well as in connection with the Old Testament, the churches came to realize that these records of apostolic tradition, with its one witness to the revelation, were not so simple and unambiguous as many Christians expected that they would be. The Rule of Faith or Truth had taken the form of what Latins called an "instrumentum," or decisive record, which looked indecisive; apparently it had some disadvantages for catholic Christians who were keenly sensitive to the need for unity of belief about their one and only Lord.

138

Inconsistencies between the Old Testament and the New were soon noticed, though the internal inconsistencies of the Old Testament appear to have attracted little attention in the Church. It was the internal inconsistencies of the New Testament which were most felt by critical students and by simple readers, especially in connection with the fourfold gospel. Once the four Gospel books were selected, probably by the churches of Asia Minor early in the second century, people were often embarrassed by the various records of the resurrection appearances, for example, or by the double genealogy of Jesus. It was the combination of the four Gospels in one collection, instead of circulating in different local churches, that created the problem; then the faithful became conscious, sometimes through outside criticism[16] but originally through private reading, that there were awkward discrepancies and varieties in the canonical records of Jesus. If Jesus was the same, why were not the stories about him the same? Was the gospel account correct in details, in order, and in contents? Or had there been primitive corruptions of the text? It is curious that the perplexity did not arise out of any sense of theological differences between the Gospels, except in the case of the Fourth Gospel as compared with the other three. The

---

[16] Striking examples of this, due to some acute Neoplatonists, are furnished by *The Apocriticus of Macarius Magnes* (especially ii. 12, 13) in the fourth or the early fifth century, where the writer attempts to answer disparaging criticisms of Christ and the gospel narratives. The English reader now has access to this document in Dr. T. W. Crafer's edition (London, S. P. C. K., 1919).

139

general ground for uneasiness lay in the fact that stories and sayings of the Lord were reported differently. By the middle of the second century this feeling was widespread, and it did not cease to haunt the minds of the faithful. So much so, that Bishop Irenaeus in Gaul of the northwest and the presbyter Origen at Alexandria and Caesarea were alarmed to find that some Christians were falling back on one or other of the four alone, not simply as their favorite Gospel but as the sole authentic witness to what Jesus had said and done. This had been the line taken by Marcion, when he chose to base his new theology on a revised edition of Luke. It simplified matters, but these two responsible Christian leaders feared that it would reduce the faith, even for members of the true Church. Efforts were made to meet the emergency by offering interpretations, more or less allegorical, which blended the differences into a plausible unity. None did this more ingeniously than Origen himself, in his desire to restore confidence in the fourfold witness of the evangelists to the one Jesus of history and faith.

Another line followed was to solve the problem by means of harmonies which arranged the material of the gospel tradition in a single sequence or running narrative. No harmony was so successful, and none is so interesting, as that drawn up at Rome before the last quarter of the second century by Tatian, a Syrian pupil of Justin Martyr. It may have been based on some Latin epitome of the gospel story which was cur-

rent at Rome. At any rate this scholar compiled his Diatessaron for members of the Church, and took it back to his native land of Mesopotamia, where it was translated from Greek into Syriac and became so popular that for over two hundred years it had the honor of being the gospel-book of the national church, to the exclusion of the four canonical Gospels themselves. Many Christians indeed continued to read the four separate Gospels in private. But at Edessa and elsewhere thousands rejoiced in a continuous narrative of Jesus which had no needless repetitions or conflicting details to distract their minds. They could now hear church lessons about their Lord without being confused or disturbed by divergent records. Not that Tatian left out all the differences; although no copy of the original survives, from versions of the Diatessaron we know that he was content, for example, to give both accounts of the birth of Jesus. Still the manual provided Christians with the essential features of one and the same Jesus for their faith and worship. Even after it was ultimately displaced from honor in the first quarter of the fifth century, when the Syrian authorities reverted to the catholic practice of using the four Gospels as they stood in the canon, the vogue of Tatian's handbook continued, through translations into Latin, Armenian, and Arabic, as well as later into Old High German and Dutch. It became the precursor of similar though less radical attempts in the later Middle Ages, some devotional and others more

141

scholarly, but all inspired by the desire and need to bring out the unity of what Jesus was believed to have been and done and taught.

About the time when Tatian's manual was being superseded in the Syrian church, the great African bishop of Hippo wrote an elaborate treatise on the Consensus or agreement of the Gospels. It is not one of Augustine's strongest works; he had not the scholarship necessary for such a task. But it reflects the sort of biblical difficulties which were being felt by thoughtful Christians, especially in view of criticisms passed by outsiders who had begun to discredit the sacred book of the Church, ever since the Neoplatonists, under Hierocles and Porphyry, had adopted this line of anti-Christian propaganda on behalf of the State.[17] Such criticism was not confined to the New Testament, of course; it included the Old Testament. But the main target was the character of Christ as reproduced in the four Gospels, which were closely studied with a view to undermine their accuracy and authenticity; Christianity, it was urged, had a wise founder, but his reporters were blundering writers. Men like Augustine and Jerome, however, had not quite the same end in view as Macarius Magnes, whoever he was. They were primarily concerned with the difficulties of ordinary Christians in the study of the Bible, who read the Gospels for themselves and won-

---

[17] The best study of the book is by H. J. Vogels in Bardenhewer's *Biblische Studien*, xiii. 5 (1908).

dered why the one Lord was not reported in one
authoritative record by the evangelists. The answer
was variously given, sometimes by explaining that the
discrepancies were more apparent than real, sometimes
by pointing out that verbal differences did not affect
the unity of the faith, and sometimes by efforts to correct the text or to show that one evangelist amplified
his predecessors. What underlay all such answers was
the fact that the Church maintained the canon of the
four Gospels, and that it was convinced of the need to
set forth their common witness to the one Lord as
more vital than their idiosyncrasies of style and statement. How this was managed may be gathered from
the sermons of a great preacher like Chrysostom and
also from the evidence of manuscripts and versions,
especially the Old Latin and the Syriac, where textual
criticism yields interesting evidence of a widespread
concern for unison, as a copyist or editor would sometimes bring one Gospel, commonly one of the synoptic
Gospels, into line with one or more of the others by
altering or omitting a phrase or more frequently by
adding something to the text.

v

One or two salient specimens may be selected to
show the methods followed. A story was current in
primitive days of an interview between Jesus and a
wealthy man. In one Jewish Christian Gospel, known
as the Gospel according to the Hebrews, the tradition

mentioned two wealthy men, though the extant fragment, which is only preserved in a Latin version, happens to begin with what the second of the two said to Jesus. "The other rich man said to him, Master, what good thing am I to do, to live? He said to him, Man, do the law and the prophets. He answered him, But I have done them. He said to him, Go, sell all you possess and divide it among the poor; and come, follow me. But the rich man began to scratch his head, and was displeased. And the Lord said to him, How can you say, I have done the law and the prophets, when it is written in the law, You shall love your neighbor as yourself? And behold, many of your brethren, sons of Abraham, are clad in filth, dying of hunger, while your house is full of many good things; and not a single thing goes out to them. Then turning to his disciple Simon who sat beside him, he said, Simon, son of John, it is easier for a camel to enter through a needle's eye than for a rich man to enter the kingdom of heaven." This vivid version did not get into the canon. The other three forms of the story are of one type, but they have their own differences. One makes the man a ruler or man of some authority in local Jewry. Another makes him a young man. One story places the scene on the road; the two others suggest that it may have taken place indoors. But most important of all is the fact that Mark, followed by Luke, begins by recording the inquirer's question thus: "Good Master, what am I to do to gain eternal life?" while Matthew has it, "Master,

144

what good thing am I to do to get eternal life?" He wanted a footing in the New Age or order which he had heard Jesus promising.[18] The reply of Jesus naturally varies; in the first version it is, "Why call me good?" In the second, "Why ask me about what is good?" Did Matthew retell the story in order to avoid the suggestion either that Jesus disclaimed moral perfection, or that he could be contrasted with God? If not, did Jesus speak both words one after another in the course of a longer conversation? The latter expedient was suggested by Augustine.[19] Indeed one Syriac version, the Curetonian, actually added Matthew's words to those of Luke. On the other hand, despite the prestige of Matthew's Gospel, some texts and versions soon preferred to assimilate it to the tradition as worded by Mark and Luke. Nor was this all, for Matthew's version of what Jesus said to the inquirer about the essential requirements of the law ended, "You shall love your neighbor as yourself," which Origen frankly proposed to omit as an irrelevant addition, inserted by some unintelligent scribe; besides, he added, Mark and Luke would never have left it out if it had been in the original. Finally, in Matthew's account of the crucifixion, the words, "another [bystander] taking a spear pierced his side, and out came water and blood," were inserted by a number of early texts and by some ver-

---

[18] So Professor Burkitt in the *Zeitschrift für neutestamentliche Wissenschaft* (1911), p. 230.

[19] It appears to be shared by Dr. B. B. Warfield, in his learned study of the whole passage (*Christology and Criticism*, pp. 97-145).

145

sions, reflecting circles of the early Church which remembered an almost similar phrase in the Johannine tradition.

Attempts to assimilate Mark's text were minor and generally unhappy. Thus, to give but two examples, Jesus was asked for an explanation of his first parable by "those who were about him with the twelve." But some churches changed Mark's phrase into "his disciples," partly because the shorter form occurred in Matthew and Luke, and partly also because (as these two later writers had already felt) the twelve alone were supposed to be worthy of receiving such a disclosure. Again, Mark records the only occasion on which Jesus blessed anyone; it was when he insisted on receiving some little children who had been brought to him, and embraced or "put his arms round" the unconscious infants. But a few texts (like D, the Sinaitic Syriac version, and some Old Latin manuscripts) removed this graphic touch in favor of the bare words "he called them," which were borrowed from Luke.

It was to prevent misconception that the divine imprimatur at the baptism of Jesus was soon altered from what Luke had written ("this day I have begotten thee") into the usual form, current in Matthew and Mark ("in thee I am well pleased," or "on thee have I set my approval"). In some churches of the West, as we learn from half a dozen Old Latin texts as well as from Ambrose of Milan's episcopal exposition of Luke, the Lucan order of the temptations was actually changed to Matthew's. Similarly church editors who remembered their Mark and Matthew often omitted "daily" from Luke's version of the demand, "let a man take up his cross daily and follow me." On the other hand it is probable or at least possible, as some manuscripts of the Old Latin version suggest, that the conclusion of Luke's story about Peter's denial ("and Peter went out and wept bitterly") was simply taken over from Matthew by editors who desired to round off the incident.

The less common tendency to assimilate John's text to the other three may be illustrated by the wonder story of how Jesus once fed a crowd of five thousand people, a tale for which the only precedents then were in Hebrew legends. It is the one story of the Galilean mission which is recorded by all four Gospels, but their interpretations differ. In Matthew Jesus first heals their sick folk; in Mark he begins by teaching them. Both evangelists attribute this to his pity, and the strange thing is that Luke, who generally stresses the humane kindliness of Jesus, leaves out this feature here, though he makes the Lord both heal and teach. The idea that an evangelist imposed his particular interests upon the tradition at all costs is untenable in the light of evidence like this, as well as in view of the further fact that Mark, who relatively speaking has less about the teaching of Jesus than the other three, introduces the incident by telling how "out of pity for them, as they were like sheep without a shepherd,"

147

people neglected by the religious authorities and without proper spiritual guidance, "he proceeded to teach them." The Fourth evangelist is only interested in the feeding, which becomes a definite sign or symbol of Christ as the bread of Life, although, as the subsequent speech indicates, this does not exclude the idea of the Lord's words[20] as the saving wisdom or revelation of God. In the wake of this special interpretation it becomes intelligible why all the first three Gospels record that the bread is distributed through the disciples, whereas in the Fourth Gospel Jesus, who takes the initiative, hands the bread himself to the people; the feeding illustrates the action at the eucharist. Still, for all such variations, it is the same Jesus who lives to satisfy the needs of men in soul and body. The differences in detail, as one evangelist after another handled the primitive tradition, were too sharply marked to permit of any artificial harmonizing here, except at a couple of minor points in the text of John. From some early manuscripts, to which the Koridethi text now falls to be added, we find there were churches which inserted the synoptic function of the disciples; instead of "he distributed" they read, "he distributed to the disciples, and the disciples to" the crowd. Then, after all was over, Mark and Matthew tell how Jesus "went back into the hills to pray by himself." The Fourth

---

[20] A significant emphasis on this occurs in the *Apocriticus* (iii. 23) of Macarius Magnes: he had come across pagans who were shocked to read "whoso eateth my flesh and drinketh my blood hath eternal life."

evangelist simply said, "he withdrew to the hills by himself"; which was natural enough, as that Gospel tends to omit almost entirely the prayer life of the Lord as inconsistent with his exalted consciousness of God. But in some quarters of the Church, as we see from Tatian's Diatessaron and codex Bezae,[21] people preferred to read, "he withdrew to the hills by himself, and there he prayed."

Two minor cases of assimilation occur in the Passion narrative of John. Some churches in Egypt, as we may infer from the Koridethi type of text, read not "vinegar" but "vinegar mixed with gall," in order to identify the drink offered to Jesus on the cross with that described by Matthew; while the discrepancy between Mark's hour for the beginning of the crucifixion ("it was the third hour") and John's tradition that "it was about the sixth hour" caused such serious discussion in the early Church that in some circles John's text was boldly altered to "third."

When differences were too sharp to be smoothed out by any correction of the text, however, preachers had to do their best to explain them away. One favorite line was laid down by Augustine. Thus, Mark tells how the disciples in the storm woke Jesus up by shouting, "Master, do you not care if we drown?" Luke

---

[21] The extent and the precise significance of these harmonizing touches is a nice problem of criticism. For this particular manuscript there is a valuable essay by H. J. Vogels on "Die Harmonistik im Evangelientext des Codex Cantabrigiensis" in the thirty-sixth volume of the *Texte und Untersuchungen* (1910).

wrote, "Master, master, we are drowning." Matthew, who often modifies phrases that seem to reflect upon the disciples, puts it, "Help, Lord, we are drowning." But for Augustine Matthew's Gospel was chief of the three, so that he could not explain the difference in this way; he merely points out that all three cries really mean the same thing, and that it does not matter which is most likely to have been uttered in the moment of panic. Besides, probably one said one thing, another said another. Which is sensible, if not to the point here. So, in dealing with Matthew's duplicates, Augustine is not perturbed. Were there two lunatics at Gadara or only one? And two blind men at Jericho or only one? There were two, as Matthew reports, but one was more prominent than the other, and so Mark and Luke merely mention him. On the vexed question whether Jesus cleansed the temple at the beginning of his ministry or at the end, Augustine declares that this was done twice, though it was only once recorded in each Gospel.

vi

We no longer attempt to reach unity in our view of Jesus by any such naïve harmonization of the texts. We find help in studying the New Testament writings apart as well as together. The science of literary and textual criticism is rather disposed not only to welcome discrepant traditions but to believe that some of the harmonizing expedients may have been in operation

150

prior to the formation of the canonical Gospels themselves. Variants become illuminating. So far from endeavoring to obliterate or to minimize the idiosyncrasies of the gospel writers, sound research rather seeks to discriminate between the different levels of reliability and different stages of insight reflected in the various traditions, showing how these might naturally arise out of various interests and by later interpretation of earlier data. Some changes turn out to be intentional, due to tendency. Others are accidental, in some cases perhaps due to different renderings of an Aramaic original. Full justice is now done to the prepossessions of the evangelists, writing for communities of different provinces and in different periods. These, it is recognized, serve to bring out a fuller historical appreciation of how some writers saw what others missed, or stressed features in the character of Jesus which did not happen to appeal to their fellows or predecessors. What New Testament criticism does is a twofold task—to indicate that different people may use different modes of interpretation in order to express a common conviction, and also to show that they may use the same or similar terms for very different objects. These varieties of argument or storytelling may be almost simultaneous, or they may be the result of deeper reflection and longer experience. Much depends upon the individual temperament, or upon the historical environment, or upon inherited beliefs. To change the figure, we might say that the New Testament Epistles, as well

151

as the Gospels, exhibit a natural tendency to sing in harmony but not in unison. Their witness to Jesus is spontaneous because it echoes such a variety of interest. But what the writers attest in very different degrees is the distinctiveness of Christianity from the start as a religion based on the fact that God in Christ had opened to men, as never before, the saving reality of his nature, in a fullness to which neither myths nor philosophy, nor even the deeper experiences of the faithful within Israel, had been able to attain.

With regard to the Gospels in particular, the issues confronting early Christians, as their movement carried them into expected situations, are indeed reflected in the accounts of Jesus which they drew up for their guidance. It is necessary and it is possible with care to determine some of these reflections in the shape and color of such stories and sayings as tradition has preserved about his earthly life, even when these turn out to be definitely symbolic, provided that one recognizes the distinction between a symbol presented in realistic garb and a symbolic suggestion shimmering through some narrative of what was originally an actual incident. Similarly with the categories for Jesus in both Gospels and Epistles. Phrases like "the Son of man" and "the kingdom of heaven" are on the lips of Jesus in the synoptic tradition, but Paul preferred other titles for the Lord's position and mission; he dropped the former, unless "the man from heaven" is an equivalent. As for the kingdom metaphor, which

152

the apostle rarely employs, the Fourth evangelist, who lived in an age when this truth had to be otherwise expressed, only uses it twice; once it is spoken by Jesus to an educated Jew, once to a pagan official, and both times it is unimpressive or misunderstood. The evangelist chose the less ambiguous and less political conception of God's household, in order to bring out the same truth of life lived in obedience and confidence to God. One or two at the outset thought of Jesus as "the Just One," a term for God or messiah; he was preached as the Just One who had been so unjustly put to death. Others drew upon the idea of the Wisdom of God in order to represent the functions of Christ; the Fourth evangelist deliberately avoided it, probably on account of its gnostic associations in contemporary life. The variety of interpretations is as unmistakable as the fact that all are elicited by the one personality of Jesus. Originally his adherents were conscious of him in the rôle of the Coming One, who was to redeem God's Israel or People, as the means of realizing the divine rule over mankind. It may be asked why the expressions of this ancient hope, drawing upon such a variety of earlier anticipations, did not gather round some other figure of the day? Why was Jesus of Nazareth chosen to be the embodiment or representative of this expectation, instead of John the baptizer, for example, round whom the later Mandaeans seem to have woven their new religion? Why, even in connection with Jesus, did the medley of pre-Christian expectations

153

never become incoherent and inconsistent? These are pertinent questions for those who prefer speculative theories about the rise of Christianity to the essential tradition of the Gospels. The one reasonable answer lies in recognizing a decisive, determining force within the personality of Jesus himself. Without a historical sense of this in its richness, as the contemporary Christian documents serve to reveal it, the origin and growth of the faith in its first phase is not soluble. What he was believed to be, he had believed himself to be—and more.

One of the enduring impressions made upon the mind by any study of history is that there is no such thing as a normal world. Similarly we have to remind ourselves that while Paul's Epistles occupy more space than the other writings of the New Testament, except the Gospels, they do not represent the normal Christianity of the first century. He was the first thinker in Christianity. His letters reveal a rich world of thought and experience, but there were other worlds of interpretation. We cannot assume that all his contemporaries thought of Jesus exactly as he did, nor even that those in his own churches shared his full mind on this matter. Indeed we know that they did not. Some disliked his theology. Some found "things hard to be understood" in their "beloved brother Paul." Still he and they owned allegiance to the same Lord. This common loyalty to Christ took various forms, but it ran deeper than all differences of thought and practice. In his own case it presupposed more than interest in Jesus the Lord as essential to his interpretation of the faith. There was deep insight into the character of Jesus. In fact it has been held that the apostle might have learned this in part before he became a Christian. "Never surely did such a controversialist, such a master of sarcasm and invective, commend with such manifest sincerity and such persuasive emotion, the qualities of meekness and gentleness." Such is Matthew Arnold's judgment.[22] "We cannot but believe that into this spirit the characteristic doctrines of Jesus, whom, except in vision he had never seen, but who was in every one's words and thoughts, the teacher who was mild and lowly in heart, who said that the last should often be first, that the exercise of lordship and dominion had nothing in them desirable, sank down and worked there even before Paul ceased to persecute, and had no small part in getting him ready for the crisis of conversion." Be this as it may, whether he had "known Christ after the flesh" in the sense of a particular acquaintance with his personality, the Jesus whom Paul knew as Lord was anything but a pre-existent being whose figure and functions were reflected from apocalyptic speculation upon vague traditions about an historical individual called Jesus. It was the same Jesus as Saint Peter interpreted in the higher messian-

---

[22] *St. Paul and Protestantism* (chap. i) ; similarly C. A. A. Scott, *Living Issues in the New Testament* (chap. i), and J. Weiss, *The History of Primitive Christianity*, ii, pp. 452f.

ism of his Epistle, independently, the same Jesus as Saint James, or whoever seems to have written in his name, hailed as Lord, from traditions of the Wisdom literature.

Probably for many at the present day it is no longer a supposed transformation of the historical Jesus into a Pauline Christ that rouses so much difficulty as the divergence between the first three Gospels and the Fourth. Recent research has indeed drawn the four Gospels together by a recognition that there is more historical tradition in the Fourth than used to be imagined. Also, "John," the third great thinker of the period, as the author of Hebrews was the second, turns out to be often using motifs already sounded in the Marcan tradition of Jesus. Furthermore, it is pointed out that the real distinction between the synoptic Gospels and the Fourth lies in the amount or degree of interpretation. Clement of Alexandria once called John's Gospel "the spiritual gospel." He really meant "the allegorical Gospel," in opposition to the literal records of the earlier three, and we now know that the latter were not literal transcripts. To some extent, indeed, apart from the Alexandrian method of exegesis, there is truth in this estimate; the Fourth Gospel does correspond to Deuteronomy in the Old Testament with its deeper interpretation of stories in earlier books of the Pentateuch. Still, the figure of Jesus in the Fourth Gospel continues to force the question, "Which Jesus?" Puzzled readers ask, "Are we to believe in

156

the synoptic Jesus or in the Johannine?" It is right to say that this is another of the false alternatives which are as mischievous in history as in philosophy. But who has the right to say this? Only one who has first done justice to the differences, instead of viewing the four books on the same plane of historicity and ignoring the special purpose of the great thinker whom we call Saint John or the Fourth evangelist. If we are not to see another Jesus in the Fourth Gospel, or if we are to avoid using all the four to form a composite picture which will not satisfy a candid view of the subject, the one recourse is to employ the historical method of differences.

It may seem a minor detail in this connection, but, although it is convenient to speak about the Fourth Gospel, the habit is misleading, for this number does not denote invariably its position in the lists of the early Church. We now learn from manuscripts and versions as well as from incidental allusions that in some churches of the West, as well as of the East, almost as early as the second century, John's Gospel was second only to Matthew, and sometimes first among the four in the order of the canon. It is not even certain that this Gospel was the fourth in order of composition; it may well have been composed about the same time as Luke's in the last decade of the first century. The reason for putting it first or second in order was occasionally the belief that it had been composed by the apostle John; of the others, only Matthew's Gospel was

believed to have been written directly by an apostle, except Peter's, which is written in the first person, and the Gospel of Peter failed to establish itself in catholic usage. Another reason was its stress on the divine nature of Jesus Christ. This commended it not only to some philosophic idealists like the Gnostics but to the Catholic Church, in an age when the supreme interest lay in that belief. Its very opening, "In the beginning was the Word," also made its continuity with the Old Testament revelation perhaps more telling than the genealogy in Matthew, since the vital tie between the Old Testament and the New Testament was another burning issue of the period. Even when it was ranked fourth in order, it was held to supplement and complete the earlier three. To us moderns its divergences from them are more apparent and perplexing, until we see it in its perspective; then they become illuminating to those who recognize that this Gospel is not on the same level of historical interest as its predecessors, but embodies a meditation or interpretation, one of whose motives is to show that recent progress in Christian thought and expansion beyond the local limits of the Founder, so far from meaning an eclipse of his career or an improvement upon his plans, was in reality their outcome.

vii

Sometimes, one must admit, the representation is so different that it is not easy to imagine how the various

158

writers can be thinking of the same Lord. The light seems to have broken into such a variety of rays that their common source becomes doubtful. This is because each representation is partial, in the sense that it is drawn from some special, urgent angle of interest. Christianity did not start with a program. For the first period the interest lay in seeing Jesus Christ as one who had really suffered, died, and risen. Many were content to think of him as the Just or the Servant of the Lord. Soon he was to return from heaven to earth, but, during the interval of waiting for his messianic reappearance, it was enough to know that he had risen, and why he had risen. Hardly anyone required to be told that he had been Jesus of Nazareth. However, when the mission broadened from Palestine into the wider world, where Aramaic required to be put into Greek, when the second generation rose, and when the expectation of a speedy (because sure) return ceased to be so deeply felt in some circles, the desire came for more information about his life prior to his last days on earth; recollections of his teaching, which had been always cherished, and tales of his career, were put into writing; these acquired more prominence than ever, as men felt that the Master had been greater than his immediate followers at first realized. The strata of tradition, though early, are neither homogeneous nor of equal value. How he was born, where he went about doing good, how long his ministry lasted—on these and other details we possess no uniform tradition, and per-

159

haps no reliable or precise information. This saying or that has been modified by subsequent reflection or experience on the part of those who preserved it. Occasionally the Lord was misunderstood or misreported. Now and then his divine authority has been underlined, till the expressions suggest more than the original story conveyed. Nevertheless it is not inaccurate to argue that lineaments of the same face appear through all the cross-lights; and it is the face of the Son of God, not of a deified hero, much less of a vague personality who could be shaped into a sort of personal guarantee for beliefs of any community which called itself Christian. The fresh traditions of the faith are ultimately derived from the impression made by an outstanding personality, transmitted by men who were in touch with him, and richly developed by contact with the larger world of thought and action. The half-century which witnessed the rise of the written Gospels was a period of which we know comparatively little, so far as the history of the Church is concerned, but it was one in which much happened. From their pages we may deduce some of the changes that had been and still were passing over the movement, as well as the different impressions made on various minds by the living tradition of the Founder's single person. Yet there is no change at the vital center of belief. Indeed it is only against the background of a common and continuous faith in Christ that the different appreciations and estimates of his life become intelligible and visible.

The common desire of the writers, whether of Gospels or of Epistles, is to see Jesus, i. e., to be in personal, direct touch with him, or to help others to enjoy this fellowship, not to see him in any detached, objective sense. As one of them put it, the aim is to be enlightened or illuminated with "the knowledge of God's glory in the face of Christ," or, as another expressed it, to "run our course steadily, our eyes fixed upon Jesus." "It is of what existed from the very beginning, of what we heard with our ears, of what we saw with our eyes, of what we witnessed and touched with our own hands, it is of the Word of Life, of what we saw and heard, that we bring you word, so that you may share our fellowship; and our fellowship is with the Father and with his Son Jesus Christ. . . . We know that the Son of God has come, and has given us insight to know him who is the real God; and we are in him who is real, even in his Son Jesus Christ." This is the keynote of the New Testament. By trained sensitiveness to this, above all things, the book is best understood. A secular musician may analyze and admire the technique of Bach's B Minor Mass, but the Christian, whether he is a musician or merely a hearer of the music, is aware of its profound religious significance; he knows that he is not reading this into the rhythms, for Bach composed the piece in order to express and transmit the central belief of Christendom. Any appreciation of the B Minor Mass is inadequate if it fails to understand the music's purpose. Great litera-

161

ture, like that of the New Testament, has indeed the same power as that of art, whether music or painting; it evokes a vital response because it is a reality, not a flight of fancy. It illustrates the truth that in art some supreme genius may appear, never to be equaled by succeeding ages. Bach will never be out of date. Neither will Raphael. So the revelation of Jesus in the New Testament is a unique embodiment of God's purpose, which possesses a timeless significance within its historical limitations of the first century. Its appearance is unaccountable, even after historical research has accounted for this and that in its environment. Yet it is only this revelation which accounts for the wealth of interpretation and for the historical activity of the faith which it evoked. There is not any other hypothesis that explains how Jesus spoke words to his time which have appealed to all time, with such inexhaustible meaning for the receptive.

viii

The historical method of attending to differences in the New Testament therefore converges upon a restatement of the truth which the early Church had naïvely asserted when it spoke of the one Gospel being presented "according to" Mark, Matthew, Luke, or John. There was not only a Gospel before the Gospels but one and the same Gospel in the four Gospels. As Hippolytus of Rome explained in his preface to the New Testament, the so-called Muratorian canon, "although various cardinal truths are taught in the several books of the Gospels, yet this makes no difference to the faith of believers, since by the one guiding Spirit all things are narrated in all about the Lord's nativity, Passion, resurrection, intercourse with his disciples, and twofold coming." There are superficial and hasty methods of stating this. But no error in perspective is more serious than to represent the inner unity of the New Testament literature as factitious. Neither can that unity be dismissed as fortuitous. However and wherever the canon was formed, it is pervaded by an explicit or implicit witness to the significance of what Jesus as Lord was to God and to man.

It is interesting, of course, though for the most part antiquarian, to separate various sections of the canon and endeavor to define the provenance and special influence of these or any of these, prior to their incorporation into the collection. Literary and historical criticism has a legitimate sphere for learned guesswork here. Nevertheless what constitutes the value of the New Testament writings for the Church is their ultimate corporate function. We may endeavor to trace the origin and aim of the five or six sources of the Hexateuch, one by one, but that does not throw much light upon the influence of the Pentateuch in Jewish religion. A reconstruction of gospel sources, or an attempt to indicate how Paul's Epistles, for example, in their collected form, may have affected Christian developments in the beginning of the second century, has its

163

place. But it was the corporate collection that gave the sacred books of Christendom their real vogue and authority, and the supreme factor in the choice and arrangement of the twenty-seven writings is beyond dispute. Christianity has from the first appealed to all sorts and conditions of men. The various types preserved in the New Testament literature have their separate attractions. Some men and women are naturally Paulinists; others are mystically minded, and to them the Fourth Gospel is supremely valuable; others, again, have a realistic, synoptic sympathy—and so forth. Yet this does not affect the fact that there is a center of gravity in the New Testament writings, a steady pull upon the mind of the historian which draws him through the differences toward the center. And the center is the revelation of God not in an idea but in a person. The movement whose initial phases are reflected in this literature, with all its ramifications and tensions, cannot be accounted for except as a new life inspired by One whom all those who belonged to the fellowship instinctively called the Lord Jesus Christ. As they sought to understand and to express their faith in him, they availed themselves of several current categories which are not always harmonious; some proved richer and more satisfactory than others. The delineations do not always supplement one another. But while they are not composed by one mind, they are inspired by one mind, the mind of Christ. The writers have their idiosyncrasies, but somehow they are looking at the same Lord as he had appeared in history at a definite period and place. What they found is what we still find in their witness, not a luminous mist rising from the bogs of myth and legend till it forms a semi-human figure, but the outline of One who can be identified. The New Testament writings do not present a series of dissolving views, whose colors shift and change, with nothing substantial behind them. It is one and the same Lord whom they presuppose and depict. Their variety of interpretations, viewed by the historian of the primitive literature and life of the Church, throws even more light upon the living model than upon the different painters.

ix

It may indeed seem a contradiction in terms to speak of Jesus Christ being the same, when one thinks of the various delineations of his person, from the first century onward, especially during the past century. Theologians, artists, historians, and literary men have been drawing him, often in their own likeness, with bewildering results. Some have not been able to identify him as others saw him. The realistic or the devotional sketch of one appears to another little better than a caricature. Blake once shouted to the Church,

> "The vision of Christ which thou dost see
> Is my vision's greatest enemy;"

and any Christian who knows what Blake meant is free

165

to say the same about his vision of Christ. The views held of Jesus have not been precisely identical in all communions of the Church itself. Belief in him and belief in what he stands for, are not always the same; some have the one without the other, or with too little of the other. Even those who repeat the same credal formula may be far from agreeing about what he requires from them or has in store for them. Within the life of one individual, again, Christ comes to mean something more, or at any rate something other, than once he did in other years when life was either less experienced or more faithful. To a real extent experience alters our conceptions of what he is and what he signifies. Furthermore, a glance at modern biographies of Jesus serves to bring out the amazing differences of Christians and others rather than the identity of him whom they depict. The first impression made by such a study is that age after age has seen or imagined a Jesus who answered to its prepossessions, theological or devotional or political, and it is a natural if hasty inference that such a biography cannot be anything else than a vehicle for conveying some favorite faith of a sect or some ideal of a school, by identifying it with a representation of Jesus. On the other hand the number and variety of these estimates may leave us with another conviction, which is that no one Church ever possesses the full truth of the matter about it, and that no age exhausts the knowledge of his life.

The latter reflection is more likely to be true. Too

166

much has been sometimes made of the limitations and
defects inherent in such a line of study. Our modern
knowledge rightly criticizes the persistent, often unconscious, tendency of a period to paint the Lord as
no more than a man of its own day who anticipated its
cherished hopes and modern interests. This is a danger
and a delusion which deserves to be exposed, although
the very attempt to correct the shortcoming often ends
by providing a fresh illustration of the narrowing pre-
occupation itself. Every generation inevitably interprets Jesus in the light of its immediate situation. The
source of error lies not in doing this, however, but in
assuming that one has said the last word on the subject. In every department of knowledge each generation, as it is wise, will confess to the next,

> "Much there is that waits you we have missed;
> Much lore we leave you worth the knowing;
> Much, much has lain outside our ken."

It is the same in Christian study of what are the ultimate issues of the faith. But in so far as the generation that passes has been faithful to the heavenly vision,
it may humbly claim to have been looking in the right
direction; whatever it may have missed or miscon-
ceived in the Object of faith and practice, it ought to
have found enough to justify the transmission of an
assurance that

> This Face, so far from vanish, rather grows,
> Or decomposes but to recompose.

Even when this assurance is not heard in small, sure sketches of Jesus, it is at any rate deduced from them by wiser minds in the next generation. The best that can be done, in any age, is to be sensible that while our modern equipment is better than that of our predecessors, it is not necessarily free from limitations of another kind. No life of Jesus can ever be written which is "scientific" in the accepted and misleading sense of the term, i. e., sufficient to prove objectively what he was and did, as a preliminary to any faith. The insensitive will continue to be insensitive. Yet he can be known in a real and trustworthy degree. Christianity has never been without some vision of him, as the great contemporary of the period, living for more than the historical imagination. There are vital elements in the tradition and experience of his person which, in spite of partial and temporary expression, are common to all ages and to all that is most Christian in any one age. Certainly "we know in part," but we know, even although part of what we do know has yet to be known better. The continued study of Christ is not a hopelessly elusive and provincial occupation. It ought to yield some wider insight and closer intimacy of experience. Men may have been too dogmatic or too skeptical or too impressionistic in pursuing it at times, as some contemporary fashion of thought has been allowed to dominate their minds, and various temperaments will continue to see him from this angle and that; but it is not a vain hope that patient, frank

168

inquiry into the issue of his divine humanity, as the clue to his identity, may not only teach love for Christ to speak of him with better knowledge but also win critical knowledge to think of him with something of the personal interest which Christians are wont to call devotion to himself.

Part Four

IN THE LIGHT OF THIS CONVICTION ABOUT THE LASTING and fresh revelation in the person of Jesus Christ, it is little wonder that from the first there was a sense of glad wonder in the worshipping Church. The letters of the New Testament repeatedly break into sudden doxologies of rapture, stirred by the thought and sight of what God meant to Christians in this final, rich manifestation of his saving will. There was a lyrical note in the apostolic faith, even in its arguments about the Lord and its appeals for right thinking and conduct. The heart of these primitive believers thrilled as their mind stirred and moved. The new meaning given to life by the living Christ throbbed sometimes in the first century with a passion of adoring worship, which is voiced not only in the songs of praise but in the informal doxologies. Thus the tiny pamphlet of Saint Judas runs up at the close into a thanksgiving "to the only God our Saviour, through Jesus Christ our Lord." It was for such a glowing faith that the good Judas had been summoning the churches to contend seriously. Faith, like truth and freedom, requires to be fought for, by force of mind as well as by other moral energies; it is stable, but it is far from being a comfortable assurance on which the saints can settle down,

170

morally or mentally, as if it could never be endangered by being abused or misrepresented. There were then, as there have been since then, explanations of the faith, of "the only God our Saviour, through Jesus Christ our Lord," which failed to do justice to the man Christ Jesus or to the truth that there is no salvation except through what God is in his incarnate life. As one writer claimed, the apostles transmitted this real truth to later generations. "It was no fabricated fables that we followed when we reported to you the power and advent of our Lord Jesus Christ; we were eyewitnesses of his majesty." The result was that, whether orally or in writing, the report wakened a living response. The Christ loved and adored by those who had been in his company in Palestine was the same Lord to whom those in other lands who had "never seen him"[1] looked up with warm loyalty. It was from what the former recollected that subsequent reflection upon Jesus Christ drew priceless evidence for any deeper appreciation of his reality and significance. He lived in more than the stories that the first generation told of him; but before long these stories were shaped into a medium which transmitted warmth as well as light from his personality.

Thus in another and a fuller sense, no less vital, Jesus Christ was realized as the same, the same as he had always been. The variety of outlook within the two generations represented by the primitive literature

[1] 1 Peter i. 8.

of the faith not only reveals his identity but also points to belief in his enduring Spirit as changeless in a world of change. We read the early history of the movement and discover new formations of the gospel, yet no new gospel. The faith seems to have an assimilative power which faces fresh situations and recasts its truth without losing it. The primitive disciples had already felt this characteristic in their conviction of Jesus. He would be, they declared, as he had always been, the same, whatever happened. We moderns put this by saying that Jesus is final and eternal. By which we mean, if we are intelligent, that through the written Word, particularly though not exclusively through the Gospels, and through the fellowship of the worshipping Church, there is transmitted to faith here and now the real and availing presence of Him who is the same yesterday, today, and forever, the last and the everlasting Word of God for our world.

i

In connection with God and the things of God, some argue that everlasting is a less apt term than eternal. The one adjective suggests little more than duration, it is held, while the other carries higher associations of inherent value and essential quality. Still, in popular usage today, as in Jewish Greek prior to Christianity, eternal may be a simple equivalent for unusually long or perpetual. Perhaps it ought to be set apart for ontological service in our English, but in practice it

172

has been interchangeable with everlasting. Ordinary Christians are content to repeat in their confession, "I believe in the life everlasting," and to sing in the Te Deum, "Thou art the everlasting Son of the Father," without feeling that eternal would be a sharper antithesis to phenomenal or transient.

It is more important to mark how "the eternal God" (literally "the God of ages") has had a variety of nuances. Originally it signified "the God of old," as in "The Eternal God is thy refuge." He was the God of the people, who had been theirs from the beginning of their existence. Then a deeper conception appears in the later prophets, as in a hymn of faith by one who was a contemporary of Zeno in Athens and of Mencius in China. Rejoicing with his comrades over the defeat of some pagan power in the Orient, when God had put down the mighty from their seats and exalted humble loyalists, the prophet wrote:[2]

> "Thou didst protect and prosper steadfast souls,
>   for they rely on thee.
> Always rely upon the Lord,
>   for the Lord's strength endures."

Literally it is, "for the Lord is a rock of ages," i. e., of old and forever a sure strength. The Christian hymn, in using the phrase "rock of ages," alters the metaphor of rock in order to suggest a refuge in Jesus, but retains the thought that this divine relief is sure

---

[2] Isaiah xxvi. 3, 4.

173

and stable, unaffected by time and change. And this had been the conviction of some Hebrew prophets during and after the exile. The supreme expression[3] of it occurs in a reassurance for exiles, worn out by delays and disappointments, who doubted whether their God could or would do anything more for them. Did he still care? Had he grown tired? The prophet replies that the Lord knows when to intervene and that his resources are not exhausted; there is no withering of his interest in the tiny group of his poor loyalists beside the waters of Babylon.

> "Hast thou not known, hast thou not heard
>   that the Lord is an everlasting God,
>   the maker of the world from end to end?
> He faints not, neither is he weary,
>   his insight is unsearchable;
> Into the weary he puts power,
>   and adds new strength to the weak."

As the great Powers of the world marched and countermarched from end to end of the Orient, let the faithful be sure that they themselves were not overlooked by the almighty, everlasting God.

A similar situation brought out Habakkuk's quivering cry of confidence in the supreme and lasting might of God:

> "Art thou not the Lord from of old,
>   My God, my majestic One?—
>   Thou diest not."

---
[3] Isaiah xl. 28, 29.

174

Again, when God declared through Malachi, "I am the Lord, I change not," it meant that his purpose and law for the people were unalterable. Probably the sentence is a warning rather than a word of reassurance. But whether it is a threat to faithless Jews that he will not relax his demands, whatever they may think, or a promise that his mercy will be continued to the penitent, it is not an abstract ontological assertion of unchangeableness in the being of the Deity. This idea only began to emerge long afterward, in the philosophic mind of Philo at Alexandria. He was shocked by some thoughtless fellow Jews who insisted on reading literally the statement of Genesis, that "when God saw the wickedness of man on earth to be great, and that man's mind was never bent on anything except evil, the Lord repented that he had made man." The Greek translators had smoothed out the daring sentence by turning "the Lord repented" into "the Lord considered" (or, reflected). Philo upbraids the literalists for hesitating to accept this rendering. Could anything be more impious, he asks, than to imagine that the Unchangeable changes? How could the Creator change his mind? We must certainly read, "God reflected that he had made man."[4] Here we come upon a Jew taking a speculative interest in the idea of the Absolute and reading it into his Bible. Strictly speaking, there is no past, present, and future for Philo in the being or mind of God.

---

[4] *Quod Deus sit Immutabilis* v.

175

On the other hand, in the only New Testament passage which alludes to the unchanging God, it is his character rather than his essence which is stressed. In the admonition of Saint James to Christians under the trials of life and faith, who were tempted to blame God for tempting them or allowing them to be tempted into sin, the retort is that the heavenly Father is invariably good, with a light that knows no change of rising or setting. Had he not given Christians their new life by the gospel, "the word of truth," i. e., the revelation of his own real nature, ever true to itself? He had implanted in their faulty natures the knowledge of his lasting purpose for human life, a perfect or faultless law for man, incapable of being improved. Such is God's set purpose, a creative Word or Will which is unvarying. Whoever is frail or fickle, God remains steadfast. There is nothing flickering or capricious or unfair in his dealings with his people.

At the same time, in justice to Philo, it must be added that he made room for this line of interpretation. His interest was always in a God to be worshipped rather than in a philosophy of religion. Once indeed he wrote a treatise on The Changelessness of God, but it was in a popular tract upon Noah's Planting (xx-xxi) that he expounded what the everlasting God meant to the worshipping soul. He read how Abraham called upon the name of "the Lord, the everlasting God" (in Genesis xxi. 33). The one was the same as the other in Hebrew; to the writer the Lord was none other than

176

the God of ages. But not so to Philo, who proceeded to explain how "Lord" implied the masterful power of divine rule, evoking fear from man, whereas "the everlasting God" was equivalent to "One who is gracious, not now and then, but always and invariably, One who bestows benefits without intermission, One who causes his gracious gifts to follow each other in unceasing flow." Philo is not content to define eternity in relation to time and space; he views it here in the light of God's relation to human nature as well as to nature and matter, although, instead of drawing "the everlasting God" near to "Lord," he unfortunately prefers to distinguish them as higher and lower aspects of providence.[5]

He had been anticipated in this view of "everlasting" by Hellenistic Judaism, as Baudissin shows.[6] In books like those of the Maccabees and Baruch[7] the phrase is employed to denote God or the Lord as faithful to himself and to his people. "You have forgotten the eternal God who reared you." "Be of good cheer, my children, cry to God the Lord; for my hope is in the Eternal, that he will save you." "O Lord, Lord God, who alone suppliest every need, who alone art just and almighty and eternal, thou that savest Israel from all trouble." It was this religious conviction that prompted the faithful in a crisis to cry, "Thou who hast

---

[5] Irenaeus had a similar feeling; he describes Christians in the Epideixis (iii) as those "who fear God as Lord and love him as Father."
[6] In *Kyrios als Gottesname im Judentum* iii., pp. 700f.
[7] Baruch iv. 8, 21-22; 2 Maccabees i. 25; 3 Maccabees vi. 12.

all power and might, the Eternal, look now upon us, pity us." In the light of such usages, it is not surprising that ever since Moses Mendelssohn translated the Old Testament in the eighteenth century, "the Eternal," the One who is, has been a favorite Jewish rendering of the tetragrammaton or four-lettered title of the Hebrew Deity.

ii

This may seem remote from the New Testament data about Jesus, but it is by no means on the fringe of our subject. The figure of Jesus in history is thrown out of focus, if the Old Testament is depreciated or ignored, for any reason. When Renan started to write his "Vie de Jésus," it was not simply his visit to Palestine that prompted him, but the conviction that the life of Jesus was both the beginning of early Christianity, which he was about to study, and in a sense the climax of Israel's history. However imperfectly he understood both of these connections, his perspective was historically correct. The religious trends disclosed in the Old Testament are indispensable to a true sense of what the incarnation means. Any prejudice against a fair recognition of this preparation for the gospel vitiates the effort to understand how Jesus at once fulfilled and superseded the hope of Israel. Constantly in the synagogues the Amidah benediction was offered, beginning, "Blessed art Thou, O Lord our God and the God of our fathers, God of Abraham, God of Isaac, and God of Jacob, the great, mighty, and revered God, the most high God, who bestowest loving-kindnesses and possessest all things, who rememberest the pious deeds of the patriarchs, and in love wilt bring a redeemer to their children's children for thy name's sake." Christians saw this wistful hope realized in Jesus Christ. God had indeed visited his people; he had sent the redeemer for whom the devout had been praying. Now they could sing,

> "Blessed be the Lord, the God of Israel,
>   for he has visited and redeemed his people;
>   he has raised up a strong saviour for us."

But to have an intelligent retrospect of all that lay behind this conviction, it is necessary to allow for what had been moving in the minds of those who wrote for Hellenistic Judaism between the prophets and Philo. Owing to the fact that such writings failed to win a secure place in the canon of the synagogue or of the Church, it is not always realized, as it should be, that their conceptions of God in relation to nature and to human nature were possibly known to Jesus himself and that they certainly influenced some of his first interpreters, at least as much as any apocalyptic strand in the variegated Judaism of the first century, or any Oriental theosophy like Iranian belief.[8]

---

[8] There is no better survey of the data belonging to this complex background than in chaps. vi-x of the third volume ("Les Idées Religieuses et Morales") of M. C. F. Jean's monograph, *Le Milieu Biblique avant Jésus-Christ* (Paris, 1936).

179

One particular thread of this tradition was the idea
of God in relation to the world, through intermedi-
aries like the Word. the Spirit, Wisdom, and angels.
But the attitude toward eternity also entered into the
mind of nascent Christianity. Certainly it is at first sight
surprising that God is not called everlasting or eternal
in the New Testament, any more than in apostolic
fathers like Clement of Rome and Ignatius of Antioch.
But the same is true of some earlier scriptures like
Wisdom and Sirach, the hymnbook of the Pharisees
called The Psalms of Solomon, First Maccabees and
even Fourth Maccabees. Similarly primitive Christians spoke of salvation, glory, redemption, gospel, and
life as eternal, but never of God himself, except in an
editorial postscript to Romans. They never called
Jesus eternal. They had other ways of expressing the
truth in question, and although the Deity had been
called eternal in their sacred Book, the Greek Old
Testament, they followed the later tendency to avoid
the adjective. "Christ abideth forever" is merely a
formal belief that the messiah is to be the perpetual
regent of the divine realm, and it is put into the lips of
captious Jews; "the king eternal" of the Pauline dox-
ology is "the king of ages," a liturgical echo of the older
title for "God."[9] The adjective (*aiônios*) for "eternal"
or "everlasting," at its best, had meant not so much that
God was above time as that he was always the same to
his people, unchanging in his relation to them, never

---

[9] John xii. 34; 1 Timothy i. 17.

ceasing to be theirs. When the devout of old praised him for his unfailing aid or appealed to him for renewed succor, they called him everlasting or eternal. It had never been an honorific term for unlimited power, nor a metaphysical term for pre-existent; as a rule it lay nearer to what Christians meant by faithful. The early Church continued to use the term, but only for the things of God.

When Christians expressed their belief in Jesus Christ as eternal, it was done more widely and figuratively than by using the traditional adjective. For example, a prophet of the exile had hailed the Lord as "the First and the Last," in order to exalt his supremacy over time; no deity of the nations is to be compared with Israel's deliverer, who foretells the future which he controls. A Christian prophet applies this title instinctively to Jesus, as he stresses the all-embracing significance of the divine Son, adding the symbol of "the Beginning and the End," which had been applied by Philo to the Logos as well as by others to God himself. "I am the alpha and the omega, the First and the Last, the Beginning and the End." Again, an anonymous teacher quoted from the hundred and second psalm in order to prove the eternal pre-eminence of the Son:

"Thou didst found the earth at the beginning, O Lord,
   and the heavens are the work of thy hands;
   they shall perish, but thou remainest,
   they shall all be worn out like a garment,

181

> thou wilt roll them up like a mantle and they shall be
> > changed,
> but thou art the same,
> and thy years never fail."

Christian faith saw more in this ancient praise of God than a conviction that he outlasted the universe; the hymn had become a tribute, not only to Christ's activity at the creation of the world, but to his abiding character and function. He had been and he was far more than any angel could be.[10]

iii

One significant illustration of this happens to be furnished by the Christian use of a romantic piece of apocalypse in the book of Daniel, where the seer describes how he watched the critical state of the world toward the middle of the second century B. C.; things were apparently going from bad to worse, "until an Assize was held, when a primeval Being took his seat on the throne of justice, with robes white as snow, the hair of his head pure white like wool. . . . The court was held and the records were opened. Then I watched until the Beast was killed. . . . As for the rest of the Beasts, they were deprived of their dominion, but their lives were spared for a certain period. Then in my vision of the night I saw a figure in human form coming with the clouds of heaven, coming up to the primeval Being, before whom he was brought, and

---

[10] Isaiah xli. 4; xliv. 6; Revelation i. 17; xxii. 13; Hebrews i. 10-12.

182

from whom he received dominion, glory, and a kingdom, that all nations, races, and fold of every tongue should serve him." The figure to whom this eternal empire is assigned is subsequently explained to be "the saints of the Most High." For a time the Beast continued to have a glorious time, like the sons of Belial, "making war upon them and overcoming them"; but at last the sentence of the divine Assize was executed in favor of the Lord's loyalists.

The literal words for "a figure in human form" were "one like a son of man." By the time Christianity arose, this original symbol of God's own people, as opposed to the brute powers of paganism, had become in later tradition an individual Son of man or heavenly Being, as was the case with the suffering Servant of the Lord. Hence the use of the oracle in the early Church to suggest, as in the book of Revelation especially, the Son of man or Lord of the Church, who eventually returns in militant authority to vindicate the cause of God on earth against a fresh and final outburst of pagan irreligion. The poet-prophet actually employs touches from the description of the primeval Being in order to depict the divine Son. But the strange phrase "primeval Being" did not appeal to the New Testament prophets. The seer in Daniel was thinking of his "God of the ages" as a venerable, majestic Judge intervening at the end on behalf of those whom he had upheld from the start of their national existence; he now took action against pagans with their upstart, new

183

cults. To the Oriental mind the symbolism was natural. Greeks found no difficulty in conceiving Zeus as old and gray-bearded. Was he not the sublime patriarchal sky-god of the race? Neither did Hebrews, as they saw their ancient God in action, bringing history to a decisive end. The term "ancient of days" was put into our English Bible by the Genevan translators of 1560; but though impressively vague, it recalls old age with some associations of weakness. While a phrase like "primeval Being" suggests the root of the idea, viz., that the "ancient of days" is no recent deity, but living from of old, for this the early Church preferred equivalents like the God of our fathers, the God of Abraham, Isaac, and Jacob, the King of ages, or the Lord God almighty, which was and is and is to come.

The last of these phrases indicates how readily the Hebrew conception of eternal as primeval passed on into the larger faith of Christianity. Unlike the Greeks, who deified Eternity as *"aión,"* Jews never thought of God as eternity; eternity was his quality and character. He was eternal as he had been primeval and as he pervaded the ages of man's history.[11] So far as Israel ever thought of eternity, it was as something which lay behind or above time, disclosing itself through successive periods, as a manifestation of the transcendent God in action on behalf of his saving purpose. The apocalyptic movement connected this with a final display of divine power, and it was in terms of this belief that the

[11] J. Pedersen, *Israel*, pp. 490, 491.

184

second coming of Jesus was interpreted, especially as "eternal" was now linked to the thought of divine faithfulness and commanding authority. When primitive apocalyptic was reset, as in the Fourth Gospel and Hebrews, for example, the result was a still richer appreciation of Christ as the lasting, faithful revelation of God to man; "eternal" became an equivalent for decisive, real, and final, though it was only used of things connected with the Lord.

In medieval thought, on the other hand, speculation upon eternity turned generally upon God and the Godhead. Historical interest was rarely felt. Ever since Boethius had elaborated the Augustinian idea of eternity, it was discussed as a quality of theism. By none more profoundly than by Anselm in the meditation which he called his Proslogium (xix): "If Thou by Thine eternity wast and art and shalt be, and if the past be not the future, nor the present either past or future, how can Thine eternity be complete at all times? Or are we to say that nothing has passed from Thine eternity, so that now it is not, though once it was, and that nothing is to come as though it were not yet? Then Thou wert not yesterday, nor shalt Thou be tomorrow, but yesterday and today and tomorrow Thou art. Nay, not even art Thou yesterday and today and tomorrow, but Thou art simply, apart from all time; for yesterday and today and tomorrow are merely distinctions in time, but Thou Thyself, though nothing exists without Thee, art still Thyself neither

185

in space nor in time, but all things are in Thee; nothing comprehends Thee, but Thou comprehendest all things." There are similar statements in medieval mysticism, some equally moving. But Christianity is more than metaphysical abstractions or mystical theism, and it is with a certain relief that one turns to the last seven chapters of Nicholas of Cusa's "Vision of God," where the great cardinal ends his great argument by appealing to Jesus Christ as the one and only revelation to men of absolute reality in God.

iv

This was a return to the center of gravity in apostolic Christianity, where the finality of Christ is put in a classical phrase by the author of Hebrews. He had been speaking to the local church about the death of some leaders, and he was going on to warn his readers against novelties of a reactionary kind in the thought and practice of the faith. "Jesus Christ," he suddenly exclaims, "is the same yesterday, today, and forever." It is not merely that the Lord lives, though human leaders pass away. It is not merely that God is as near to these Christians as he had ever been to those who originally heard the gospel from the apostles, still distributing gifts of the Holy Spirit; they must not imagine that they were living in any afterglow of the true faith. The writer reaches deeper than this. He affirms that Jesus Christ is at present what he had been in his earthly life, and that he will be the same, as strong to

186

save, whatever befalls. Christ has opened the "new and living way" to God, and while that was and is ever a new experience as it is followed, nothing new can be added to it; any novel form of communion with the living God is a bypath, even though it may be put forward as a spiritual method.

While the writer of Hebrews retains the primitive idea of the Lord's return, he does not think in terms of an immediate or sudden end. Rather he seems to be conscious of a future after today, when life will be going on as it has gone on, with change after change, shaking the fabric of things on earth, and altering what was supposed to be permanent; but he is sure that there will never be any change or need for change in the final order which Jesus has initiated. For our writer the eternal is final because it is real. He interprets this in the light of Christ's character and personality. Christ is the eternal priest on account of what he was and is. He is the same yesterday, today, and forever. Consider Christ Jesus, look to Jesus. These are the writer's pleas. Attention to realities is the dominant note of his teaching, and these realities are summed up in the person of the Lord. A sustained and unwavering attention to the unwavering Christ is the theme of his great argument, in its various phases.

This was not a new thing in primitive Christianity. It is at the heart of Paul's teaching. "Seek those things which are above," the apostle wrote, using a common phrase of ethical idealism among the Greeks. The

187

things above are the things unseen, the eternal realities. But for the Church they represent the spiritual
order, as the apostle instantly explains, "where Christ
sitteth on the right hand of God." It is his presence
and divine authority which makes the unseen world
of aspiration a reality, as he is not a Christ who is
poetically or figuratively called God but the risen reigning Lord. It is he, not things, that must be considered,
he pre-eminently, who commands the attention and
obedience of the faithful in the name of God. Through
him, as Clement of Rome put it, "we gaze into the
heights of heaven." Only, in Hebrews this emphasis
upon the Lord's enduring character and function is
brought out more vividly than elsewhere in the New
Testament literature. While Christ is not explicitly
called eternal, all that is connected with Christ, salvation and redemption, inheritance and covenant, is
stamped as eternal. It is as though the writer felt not
merely that the Lord in every aspect was better than
anything in the past of religion, but that he could never
be excelled or impaired.

v

One form of change was not before the writer's
mind; the possibility of change from a higher to a lower
affection, such as may be felt in our human relationships, when a friend ceases for some reason to be what
he once was. Wordsworth had a friend who at one time
seemed for some reason to be dropping away from him.

Disturbed by the loss of his companion's intimate affection and keen interest, by what he called "a change in
the manner of a friend," he wrote some lines beginning,

> "There is a change—and I am poor;
> Your love hath been, not long ago,
> A fountain at my fond heart's door,
> Whose only business was to flow;
> And flow it did."

Whereas now the poet is conscious of a reserve and
aloofness, which had made him poor. Human life has
examples and experiences of this kind, with loyalty
waning under some strain of the relationship between
two people. But the New Testament contains no such
apprehension on the part of Christ's followers. The
only allusion to such a fear is a significant sentence in
one of the Gospels, which glories in the Lord's unfailing devotion to his group. "Now when Jesus knew
that his hour was come that he should depart out of
this world to the Father, having loved his own who
were in the world he loved them to the end." This
introduces the story of all that he said and did on the
last memorable evening and the day following; it was
remembered as an unbroken flow of his love for those
who belonged to him, proving that this knew no check
or change, little as they might deserve his favor. So
it is when another writer declares, "He ever liveth to
make intercession for" his own, or when the prayer
rose from still another group, "Grace be with all who

189

have an undying love for our Lord Jesus Christ," since
that lasting loyalty is the response to his undying love
for them in death and life. There is a human love
which does alter as it finds some altered feelings in
those who are its objects; as they prove fickle, ungrate-
ful, or indifferent, it may be withdrawn. Certain forms
of affection may be outgrown or lessened in the course
of time.

> "Space is against thee; it can part.
> Time is against thee; it can chill."

But Christians never dreamt of regarding the divine
love for them in any such connection, though they commonly thought of the Lord's lasting relation as that of
one who was true to his promises, on the lines of the
Old Testament. Charles Wesley's verse echoes this
conviction:

> "Jesus, we steadfastly believe
> The grace Thou dost this moment give
> Thou wilt the next bestow;
> Wilt keep us every moment here,
> And show thyself the Finisher,
> And never let us go."

Now and then the primitive tradition preserved some
record of his followers slipping into a panic of despair
("Carest thou not that we perish?"), but these memories were confessions, honestly repeated in order to
show how unfounded such a fear had been, and how
changes and crises had only brought out his unchang-

190

ing, unfailing interest in the group. So far from having any real reason to doubt him, the disciples were not ashamed to own that they had more than once surprised and disappointed him by misgivings about his power and will to care for them.

To some in the primitive world of Christianity, who had been living in the Roman atmosphere, this revelation of the Lord Jesus, as eternally true to his own, must have been singularly appealing. Their inherited conception of *pietas,* which was a synonym for what we call religion, amounted to a steady fulfilment of duty to gods and men, as the worshipper ordered his life by what he believed to be obedience to the divine will. These gods, who were served by ritual and prayers, were practically distinguished in popular religion from the supreme Power in a vague, semi-personified shape, when they were not left indeterminate altogether. In reading an author like Virgil, however, we find that "they are irresponsible, and even to human seeming capricious. They cannot be relied upon to make due return for the service of duty paid to them."[12] It was no wonder that some earnest souls were fascinated by the offer of the so-called mystery religions to provide the pious with a deity who had some closer, though loose, connection with a supreme deity, as in the case of Hermes or Isis and Osiris, and who above all could be relied upon to uphold their devotees with unfailing care. It was not simply that devout folk in the empire

---

[12] J. W. Mackail's note on Aeneid xii. 839.

191

thus got one sort of god who had a saving personal interest in them as individuals thirsting for immortality and freedom from fate and chance, but that this deity promised them a close relationship of intimate fellowship as well as an avenue to the presence of some ultimate, real power over the universe, such as the State religion did not provide. A worshipper of Isis, the queen of heaven, appeals to his madonna as "the holy and eternal succorer of mankind, evermore cherishing mortals with thy rich bounty."[13] The drawback was that these deities had no character in history. It was a further revelation for such men to realize what the Church held out to them when it preached a Lord who in unfading love had really lived as man on earth, entering into human conditions, dying and rising to be the changeless Lord of his own folk. The mystery cults, rooted in nature-worship, faded before very long; Gnosticism and neo-Platonism superseded them, and the belief of the Church outlived them all, that belief in Jesus the Son of God, which is implicit in the primitive tradition of Gospels and Epistles alike.

This belief after the resurrection showed Christians how God had not put Jesus so far from his followers that they could no longer hear him speak. The Church was full of people who did more than recall what he had said; they knew him as a living Lord. The Spirit moved prophets to speak in his name to the communi-

---

[13] Apuleius, *Metamorphoses,* xi. 25.

ties.   A writer like the Fourth evangelist, in thinking
of what Jesus had been, could not help being conscious
of what he was at the moment.   Another evangelist,
who began by explaining that the name "Jesus" had
been anticipated by the prophecy of Emmanuel,
"which being interpreted is, God with us," ended by
recording the final assurance of the risen Jesus to the
disciples, "Lo, I am with you always, even to the end
of the world."   It was a relationship which might be
described as a friendship that has mastered time, a
friendship that was not confined to one race or to one
age. When Frederic Myers heard Dr. Frederic Temple
preach to the boys in Rugby chapel, he was moved to
be grateful for this note in the service:

> "For, as he spoke, I knew that God was near
>   Perfecting still the immemorial plan,
> And once in Jewry and forever here
>   Loves as he loved and ends as he began."

Christian faith will not consent to do without such a
conviction about Jesus Christ.   It was a vital element
in the faith once for all delivered to the saints of the
first century, which delivered them from uncertainty
about the lasting power of their religion.

There is indeed one kind of high change suggested
by human experience of a gifted personality or a rare
spirit who impresses his contemporaries with a profound sense of further capacity.   Tennyson wrote of
his friend Hallam:

193

"For what wert thou? Some novel power
Sprang up forever at a touch,
And hope could never hope too much
In watching thee from hour to hour."

The parallel is imperfect. But it indicates the sense of
unlimited range which some New Testament writers
felt in looking to the Lord as they faced new situations,
sure that he would be more than equal to them. They
found that their faith had an answer to questions which
had not been raised in provincial Palestine. In Christ
"all the treasures of wisdom and knowledge lie hidden." His Spirit would "lead them into all the truth"
about himself; "he will draw upon what is mine and
disclose it to you." The truth of his life would never
be antiquated. "Thou shalt see greater things than
these." "He that believeth in me shall do the works
that I do; and greater still shall he do, because I go to
my Father." Or, as one preacher of the second century declared in a Christmas or Easter sermon: "God
sent the Word to appear to the world, whom the chosen
people dishonored, whom the apostles preached, and
in whom the heathen believed. The Word was from
the very beginning, appeared as new, was proved to be
old, and is ever young as he is born in the hearts of
the saints. He is the eternal One, who today is
accounted the Son, through whom the Church is
enriched and grace unfolded."[14]

---

[14] *The Epistle to Diognetus* xi. 3-5.

vi

What we meet in the pages of the New Testament is a witness to Christ in all tenses, past, present, and future. But this turns upon one Action of God which was final. We overhear one man assuring or rather reminding his readers that "Christ has once suffered for sins, the just for the unjust, that he might bring us to God," another telling how "once at the end of the world he has appeared to put away sin by the sacrifice of himself," and a third announcing, "The death he died was for sin, once for all." Once for all; it need never be repeated, it was the full, final sacrifice which ensured man's communion with God. From the very beginning, Christians believed that what the Lord has done could not be surpassed, and would not require to be supplemented. The teacher who wrote the homily to Hebrews argued this truth; whereas others had been content to reiterate or to illustrate it as an axiom of the faith, he explained it in pithy phrases. It is as though he saw the cross on Calvary in the eternal order of things; "Christ in the spirit of the eternal" or, through the eternal Spirit, "offered himself as an unblemished sacrifice to God," thereby mediating man's approach to the presence of God with a direct, real access. This raises the modern problem of how an action in history can be considered to possess final or absolute value. But the writer had not this before his mind. He simply affirms that the divine forgiveness which opens

195

up fellowship and worship fully, was at once a single action and also of eternal moment to mankind. What helped to make his argument telling was the fact that he and his fellows took sin seriously, as a defiance of God, as an offense against God, or as a violation of God's law. A saying like that about "the spirit of the eternal" sounds as Platonic as anything in the New Testament, but it rose from a profound Hebraic sense of sin, though Christians advanced beyond Jewish theism in recognizing that the revelation of Christ pointed to self-sacrificial love at the heart of God's forgiveness. Furthermore, Christians have only one day of Atonement, and it is not annual. The human life of Christ, with its suffering, death, and resurrection, was but an interlude in his eternal existence, which availed for all time because it was in time and yet not temporal.

This is illustrated by what happened when some primitive Christians, like the authors of the Pastoral Epistles and Second Clement, took over the Greek religious term "epiphany," which ever since the period of the Maccabees had been used in Hellenistic Judaism for some divine interposition on behalf of God's people in a crisis. In the Greek Orient it had come to denote the manifestation of a god whose coming was supposed to shine at the accession of some monarch from whom saving aid was expected on earth. An epiphany was in one way or another the dawning of divine light and favor for a darkened earth. In the worship of Dionysus it meant the repeated reappearance of the god ascend-

196

ing from the lower world. Such ethnic usages were a dim anticipation of the truth and hope that the dominant characteristic of the divine nature was to be helpful, or in a sense gracious. But when men in the Church first employed the word, they were conscious that while their Lord's career had been a manifestation of God in aid of his people, it was not an "epiphany" in the current sense of the term. We may call the sudden appearances of Jesus between the death and the ascension "epiphanies," but the early Christians did not. The term, five times out of six within the New Testament, signifies the expected return of Christ in glory, not his earthly life, not even any miraculous action in that life. Only once is it applied to the first advent of the Lord to this world of need and sorrow, and even here it is not connected with a definite act of help or healing but with God's grace "revealed in the appearance of our Saviour Jesus Christ, who has put down death and brought life and immortality to light by the gospel" of the reigning, risen Lord who had once for all visited the human sphere. Elsewhere the appearance or epiphany of his divine power as incarnate is displayed pre-eminently in the climax of the resurrection, with its hope of the Lord's return in full power to crush finally the powers of evil and thus complete the saving purpose of God for his people. Here the belief is expressed in terms of the Hellenistic idea that the yearning for immortality could only be satisfied by some divine illumination; but in Chris-

197

tianity the illumination was the real personality of Christ, and the appearance was once for all, whether the stress fell on the first or on the second coming.

One expression for this truth is to call him unique. Now "unique" may not be a very happy or useful term in this connection; it may mean too much or too little, either that Jesus is sharply distinguished from the human race, different in kind as well as in degree, or that he is unique as any individual is. A personality, especially a great personality, is always unique, in the sense that he is himself. But it is not unfair to call the Lord unique in the sense that his life was not one among many. His function was unparalleled and pre-eminent. What he was and what he did cannot be removed or improved. This was what early Christians meant when in language of their own they hailed him as "the same" forever. It is not as though there were an unlimited disparity between him and us. Then he could be of no value to us. Nothing in Nature, nothing even in the nature of God, can be out of relation to us. Christ's life came in the line of a revelation already experienced from time to time in the Hebrew and Jewish phases of the People of God. There was a full recognition by his first interpreters of how he had inherited as well as recast some of the great traditions of the past. His coming was never, except by the Marcionites, conceived as a sudden afterthought of God, unrelated to Israel and the moral order. There was continuity. But there was something more than a

198

remarkable development in his person; there was something incomparable, original, creative as well as created. People have often talked of Christianity as an evolution, forgetful of the subtle error that besets any transference of scientific categories into a realm of volition where they are irrelevant. It is more intelligent to recall how, as has been already noted, the creation of the gospel-stories, which are an embodiment of Christ's being, resembles supreme art rather than science. For in the flowering eras of such art, whether painting or music or sculpture or architecture or literature, classical masterpieces are born which cannot be accounted for by any mere analysis of antecedent conditions or contemporary tendencies, masterpieces that survive any subsequent period of decline and devitalization, only to awaken wonder and response from ages to come. They are not subject to reaction. Later ages cannot hope to excel them. All that can be done by posterity is to understand them better, to enter with finer sympathy into their spirit, and to realize their power more fully.

Here the faith of Christendom naturally encounters the need for some philosophy of history, as no other religion requires to do, and perhaps at the present day more acutely than at any period since Augustine wrote the "De Civitate Dei." The religious convictions of the Church are faced by the difficulty of expressing themselves in such terms as modern metaphysics on the one side and historical science on the other will permit. There is also the challenge tabled by philosophies of the Absolute or of the State. Yet the convictions amount to one paramount issue. What differentiates Christianity from other religions is its belief about Jesus Christ, the Son of God. "God was in Christ, reconciling the world to himself." "This is life eternal, to know thee, the only true God, and Jesus Christ whom thou hast sent." "You believe in God; believe also in me." In such simple sentences the Christian claim to be final and absolute is quietly voiced. Here lies the decisive issue, beside which all others are comparatively minor. To be aware of it, however imperfectly, is to be in the proper focus for understanding Jesus. Otherwise, when his divine humanity and his vital relation to the believing fellowship are treated as extras or accidental features of the legend, he remains a wavering shadow for the historical quest. It is when the mind occupies the perspective of regarding these as essential to the gospel and implicit in the traditions of the earliest Gospels, that one may address oneself to literary criticism in its broadest sense, to historical research, to an examination of the Christian tradition in its varieties and vitality, to an appreciation of the religious temper and its phenomena in other fields of human nature, past and present, and to a grasp of newer methods in psychology and metaphysics, only to find that these all enter into the process of estimating fairly the evidence for doing justice to the three truths which are enshrined in the clas-

sical literature of the New Testament, viz., that Jesus Christ lived a real, human life on earth, that he is to be, as he has always been, worshipped by those who believe in the one God, and that his revelation is final for man's faith and need.

vii

It is useful to distinguish literature of knowledge from literature of power. Yet there is literature of knowledge which is also literature of power, literature which transmits truth so effectively that it continues to move readers of a later age whose world is no longer that of the original writer and readers, moving them not merely to admire but to act. Such is the New Testament, provided that it is not isolated from the Old Testament or from the living Church. When life is greatly moved, there is an element of reminiscence as well as of expectation. Here and now men become aware of more than their immediate experience; they are conscious of a present which flows out of a past and flows into a future. Time for Christian faith has its zigzags, but it is a moving line, the past in the present and the present in the past, both being aspects of one reality. It is not simply our past, i. e., what has happened to ourselves. It is the past of the living Church to which we belong, with its historical continuity through the ages. The Word will not allow us to forget this lasting testimony to the unchanging Lord. For there, as we read, we learn to experience

201

not only the creative Acts of God but his presence within a fellowship where we are taught to see the living God revealed through others, in our duties to them and in their examples of faith and hope. The Spirit of the incarnation carries on, through the Word within the Church, from age to age. To ignore this context means that Jesus Christ is being drawn out of scale. "Thou shalt call his name Jesus, for he shall save his people from their sins." "I speak concerning Christ and the Church," said the apostle Paul. The prophet John never mentions the Lord in heaven except in connection with the worshipping fellowship of the Church. The New Testament is for a fellowship, or for individuals belonging to that fellowship, where Jesus is Lord.

The result is that as Christians within the new fellowship read about the Lord in the Word, they find him at their side. The Word is liable to criticism, as any product of time and history must be, however classical; but it also transmits the living power of Jesus still. There is far more than information about God in its pages. Indeed it becomes "the Word." As the Scottish thinker, Thomas Erskine of Linlathen, wrote to F. D. Maurice, "There is an immense difference between hearing about God and hearing God." Or, as he put it to Miss Julia Wedgwood, "All religion is in the change from He to Thou. It is a mere abstraction as long as it is He. Only with the Thou we know God." This means the Word being read with the wor-

shipping spirit, in which it was originally written. Scripture leaves us in no doubt whether man should call God "They" or "It" or "He." Scripture moves the serious reader to call him "Thou," as it has always done; it becomes an inspiring medium of communication between God and his people.

This is so familiar that it does not require underlining, but here are two examples of how the story of Jesus reverberates with appeal to later ages. The first is taken from a tale of how Jesus, on his way north from Judea, "being weary with his journey, sat" down to rest beside a well of the Samaritans. There he talked to a local woman about the water of life, until she began to drop her offhand manner, as the stranger impressed her in spite of herself. One of her remarks to him was, "Give me this water, that I thirst not." Apparently it is no more than one of the casual[15] details in an incident connected with his unexpected mission to Samaria, but the story carried far beyond the range of its original setting. It made the same personal impression upon a man and a woman in the Italy and the Spain of later Europe, as they read the record and thought of their Lord. When an unknown Italian, possibly the Franciscan Thomas of Celano, composed his sequence on the "Dies Irae," he prayed in two

---

[15] Though early in the thirteenth century (1210-1214), when a wandering English scholar, Gervase of Tilbury, compiled a popular miscellany to amuse and edify his royal master, Otto the Fourth, he gravely explained that Jacob's Well marked the central point of the earth (*Otia Imperialia* dec. 1. § 10).

quivering stanzas which have haunted and helped thousands ever since the thirteenth century:

> "Recordare, Jesu pie,
> Quod sum causa tuae vitae,
> Ne me perdas illa die;
>
> "Quaerens me sedisti lassus,
> Redemisti crucem passus;
> Tantus labor non sit cassus."

The terse Latin defies translators, but the verses mean something like this:

> "Remember, loving Jesus, it was I
> For whom thou hadst to journey on thy way,
> Lest I be lost to thee on the last day;
>
> "In search of me thou didst sit weary, yea
> For my redeeming bore the cross and pain;
> O may such labor be not all in vain!"

Three centuries later the tale appealed to the daughter of a hidalgo in Avila. She was fascinated by a picture of the Lord at the Samaritan well which hung in her bedroom, and especially by four words underneath the canvas, "Da mihi hanc aquam"—"Give me this water." It was one of the earliest religious impressions made upon the girl who grew up to become Santa Teresa. Two centuries later, within the English Church, one discovers that a devout, unsentimental scholar, Samuel Johnson, never heard or read the second of the Latin stanzas without being moved to tears—"Quaerens me sedisti lassus . . . tantus labor non sit cassus." Nor is

204

this all. Fifty years ago, when Dean Church died, the finest humanist in the English communion of his day, it was found that he had asked to have two stanzas of the "Dies Irae" inscribed on his tombstone; one of them was

> "Quaerens me sedisti lassus,
> Redemisti crucem passus;
> Tantus labor non sit cassus."

The second example is of a simpler nature. A great Russian writer has drawn a little sketch of a divinity student warming himself at the fire in a humble cottage where he had taken shelter from the storm on his way home. Two peasant women were there, a mother and a daughter, both widows. They were strangers to him. So, to interest them and put them at their ease, he modestly began to tell the story of how the apostle Peter had once warmed himself at a fire, nineteen centuries ago, and how the Lord Jesus after being betrayed by Judas in the garden, had been three times denied by Peter. He looked up to find the women troubled and in tears over the tale, not because he had recited it quietly and naturally, but because they were absorbed in what Peter had felt, as though he were one of their own neighbors. And suddenly the student realized what had never occurred to him as he heard the gospel passage in the liturgy or studied it in the classroom. The emotion of these unlettered women was a revelation to him of how little time had to do with the gospel.

As Chekhov puts it, when the lad watched the effect of
the simple familiar story on the peasants, he had a thrill
of warm joy in realizing for the first time how the past
is linked to the present. It was as if he had seen both
ends of an unbroken chain reaching from the far-off
scene in Palestine to the cottage in Russia. As he went
home through the cold, dark night, life now seemed to
him full of mysterious hope and happiness; he was
thrilled by the thought that what had moved human
life nineteen centuries earlier in the courtyard of the
high priest at Jerusalem and in the garden of Gethsemane, had somehow continued to that day without a
break, and was evidently the supreme thing in human
life. What did time matter, he thought, compared to
this truth of truths?

So, through the written account of Jesus, as the
inner history of vital Christianity proves for nineteen
centuries, there passes into men and women, learned
and uneducated, ordinary and gifted, the realization
of his lasting, living presence; he becomes the unchanging Lord in touch with those who live in change. They
hear or they read of him, and to them he is still the
same. This "thought of Christ which has filled the
mind of the world," as Benjamin Jowett pointed out,
"has nothing to do with those microscopic inquiries
respecting the composition of the Gospels which have
so greatly exercised critics." Such investigations often
aid it, but it is not confined to the sphere of analysis
and historical reconstruction. If it is ignored in that

sphere, learned investigations prove to be secondary and superficial, from the religious point of view.

viii

This inspiring function of the Book has been so caricatured and abused by theories of ecclesiastical tradition and of verbal inspiration that, to prevent misconception, one must be careful to distinguish it from any question of later ages giving a new lease of life, as it were, to some genius of the far past in life or in literature by associating certain words of his with later interests which have become vivid and vital for the present. We are familiar with this experience. Men are heartened if they can persuade themselves that their aims have been strangely anticipated or foretold by a great figure in remote days. The sense that what they desire has been already pointed out, adds to their confidence, especially if they can appeal to a genius who was connected with their earlier history and read into his utterances a confirmation of their own dreams. This sort of interpretation does throw light upon the function and methods of the Christian tradition about Jesus. Over and again men have depicted him in the light of their prepossessions, not altogether without reason. But were this all, the center of gravity would lie in what we make of Christ, rather than in what he makes of us. For those who are sensitive to the truth of their faith, the revelation of God in Christ possesses intrinsic qualities which do start into new significance as time

207

goes on, when the facts of faith are allowed to react powerfully and freshly on the mind and conscience. This is much, but it is not everything. The relation of the written Word to the living Church means a special philosophy of inspiration like this: we may say that, as God's self-revelation enters into history and experience, to carry out his purpose and to realize his will, pre-eminently through the life of Jesus Christ on earth, the Word cannot be confined to its immediate and original audience. These recipients attest it, but they do not exhaust its significance. In their testimony lies a historical guarantee of its characteristic qualities. But also through them the revelation is transmitted; it is communicated afresh to successive generations, and Scripture or the written word is a vital factor in the process. The decisive revelation in the person of Jesus Christ must indeed be understood rightly, interpreted by obedience as well as by study, if it is not to fail in its aim. But it contains more than the first witnesses could realize, since it is an endless disclosure, and this fact goes far to determine our view of its original record by the apostolic witness which is enshrined within the New Testament. The reason, not the reason why the individual writers composed their books but the providential reason which accounts for the Word in its present form—the reason why such a record was drawn up and preserved was to enable men of later ages to enjoy in their own way an immediate personal experience of the revelation which the documents attest. As

208

Rothe put it, nearly eighty years ago, "the record of revelation can do this without fail, provided that it is really, as its name implies, the original record, that is, such a record as is itself an integral element in the revelation which it enshrines,"[16] thereby generating or doing something to generate similar religious experiences of the Lord who is its center and subject. To the Church as the Body or fellowship of the Lord, the Word is thus organic. Through both His living presence is mediated.

Naturally this is impossible unless revelation is assumed to be a direct manifestation of the living God to his people. However essential confessions of faith may be, any identification not only of the Word with the Bible but of revelation with credal decisions of the Church, throws the gospel out of focus. On the other hand there is what may be called a sacramental power in the written Word, as there has always been. Reading or hearing the Word read is a normal medium of contact with the living God. Criticism, as criticism is true, does not undermine this; it may enable the trained mind to appreciate what the devout know by intuition, disclosing evidence for a lasting, timeless power of God in the classical pages which portray the Jesus of history and of faith. This forms a valid function of Scripture. It is no use to erect some shrine of

---

[16] *Zur Dogmatik*, pp. 153f. The same argument is worked out by Dr. P.T. Forsyth in his *Person and Place of Jesus Christ* (pp. 151f.), a book which anticipates much of what is best in modern criticism of the subject.

belief on the basis of this or that idealism, and then
place, in a synthesis of the inner light, some symbolic
figure called Jesus or Christ, who may be romantically
called God, as though this availed to consecrate the
structure better than anything with a biblical representation. Men cannot adore an allegory or surrender
life to a symbol of goodness and truth. The Scriptures
of the Church are indispensable to a knowledge of the
living Lord. "God speaks to me here and now on the
basis of what He has spoken already. He speaks to
me through the holy Spirit on the basis of what He has
said in Jesus Christ. This 'has' is bound up with the
conception of the canon," since the canon, like the
primitive Church in which and for which it was created, forms an action of the Spirit; indeed it is a sphere
of the Spirit. "In order to speak to me personally
today, God makes use of what is accessible to everybody
in his actual language within the fixed Word of the
Bible, even though the Bible's revelation is not accessible to everybody,"[17] i. e., in the sense of being welcomed by all who read about it. Some contemporaries
of Jesus heard him, and were deaf or indifferent. Some
saw him, and saw nothing in him. Age after age,
within as well as outside the Church, some hear his
Word and do not understand it, because they do not
care to understand it. But the Spirit which inspired
the gospel and its record lives in the fellowship where
the Word is rightly read. This is what was meant by

---

[17] Brunner, *Natur und Gnade*, pp. 35, 36, as in *The Mediator* (pp. 431f.).

"the inward witness of the Spirit"; it does not simply guarantee the presence of an inside supernatural power in the Bible, it transmits this, not in rivalry with the Church, but within the corporate Body of Christ. In spite of exaggerations and misapplications, the activity of the Spirit is thus experienced through reading and preaching. The Word has proved to be charged with power for the sensitive who fulfill the conditions bound up with its revelation of reality.

ix

The response may be described thus. When Samuel Rogers, the English poet and banker, was admiring a life-size picture of the Lord and his disciples at the Last Supper, which hung in the refectory of a Dominican convent in Padua, an old monk remarked to him, "I have sat at my meals before it for seven and forty years and such are the changes that have taken place among us, so many have come and gone in the time, that when I look upon the company there, silent as they are, I am sometimes inclined to think that we, and not they, are the shadows." There is a deep truth in this impression. "What shadows we are, and what shadows we pursue!" an English statesman reflected, after the death of a great contemporary; the religious man reflects, "My days are like a shadow that declineth. But thou, O Lord, shalt endure for ever." For, in looking to Jesus, men also acquire a sense of their own reality, as they belong to God in him. Life may be fleeting, and men but shadows, yet in Christianity people become conscious of the great meaning and lasting significance which he has brought into the short span of their existence here. At certain moments a man

> "Knows himself no vision to himself,
> Nor the high God a vision, nor the One
> Who rose again."

Such is one effect of the Christian experience. And for this reason, among others, that an experience of this kind depends upon an Act of God, an actual happening in history. Insurance charters or contracts speak of an Act of God, meaning by that some unforeseen and violent accident. Civilization recognizes this kind of divine act alone; it is an inexplicable misfortune that befalls a project or a voyage. But Christianity knows an Act of God which is the best fortune that ever befell men. It is an Event that is an Evangel, the coming of Jesus to our world. Faith in the divine aim of this action is an experiment which ends in some personal certainty of One who is real, and the evidence for this gathers naturally as faith becomes more active and responsive to the will of the Lord. In looking thus to him, every age is doing what millions of people have done already, and what millions will continue to do, long after our particular generation has passed. If the successors of any age are to keep their minds upon Jesus, nothing will aid them like a loyal, thoughtful testimony from their predecessors, instead of a moral or mental slackness which produces a sense of unreality in the whole business of Christianity.   When Herbert Trench wrote,

> "The Man upraised on the Judean crag
>   Captains for us the war with death no more;
> His kingdom hangs as hangs the tattered flag
>   Over the tomb of a great knight of old,"

he was thinking of modern inquiries into immortality and psychical research, which seemed to promise what Christianity had failed to provide.   On that, as on some other issues of our day, a closer study of the essential truth of Christianity, under the forms of its first-century expressions, may do something to remove or relieve the fear.   But in any case misgivings about the future of the faith or about the inexhaustible power of Christ's revelation generally arise from some failure to appreciate what has been given to man in the Lord Jesus.   Whether the failure comes from an imperfect effort to appreciate what he really was or from a defective obedience to his authority, it remains true that hope for the future is likely to be active and intelligent in proportion to our historical assurance of what God once did for us men and our salvation.

That assurance is not lightly gained, but it is not out of reach.   In one of the birth stories, some wise men announced that they had traveled all the way to Palestine, because "we have seen his star in the east and are come to worship him"; then, as soon as "they saw the young child with Mary his mother, they fell down and worshiped him," offering to him their treasured gifts. One point of the tale is that these sages were living in superstitions which they never realized to be superstitions until they had put themselves to some trouble in order to see Jesus. It had cost them something to act on their intuition and to enjoy its fulfillment. In a deeper and wider sense, any clear perception of Jesus as Lord implies a moral sympathy with what we some-how imagine the will of God means in this world, and a personal readiness to act upon such indications of it as are at present accessible, even, if need be, to sacrifice prepossessions and forego satisfaction with inherited traditions in order to follow the new gleam and reach some experience of ampler worship. When Archbishop Söderblom once summoned his hearers to face the duty and opportunity of serving and seeing the will of God in contemporary civilization, he explained that he used this order of words, "serve and see," deliberately. "For in the kingdom of God no one can see so long as he remains merely a spectator. Those only who serve the will of God sacrificially can see the will of God."[18] This principle has a bearing upon any quest for a bet-ter knowledge of Jesus. Today we have seen his star in the west, but it is the same Star of the morning that draws us in search of him. Many of us are not at all wise; we are not learned except in so far as we have

---

[18] *The Nature of Revelation*, p. 168.

learned that no wisdom of life avails if it does not lead us to worship, with such light as our best knowledge is able to receive and willing to obey. We too may conceivably find that the religion of Jesus Christ is not what we had expected. Indeed at first the study of the Gospels may seem to bring us in sight of little more than

"The somewhat which we name but cannot know,
    E'en as we name a Star, and only see
His quenchless flashings forth, which ever show
    And ever hide him, but which are not He."

Yet in undergoing a critical and even a costly discipline of mind and of will in this subject of subjects, men have been rewarded eventually by some fuller recognition. The truth as it is in Jesus, like truth in any other sphere of moral or spiritual life, is more than what we are prepared to accept in the optative mood, because we would like to believe it; at every stage of the process it is what we accept with a purpose to act upon it, come what may. More than that, it is often what we accept after a struggle with prejudices as well as with passions. So alone are convictions secured, especially convictions about the Lord Jesus Christ. They are not casually picked up by dispassionate spectators of a life-and-death issue; they cannot be enjoyed by unmoved adherents of a movement. But when men and women decline to approach the study of the Lord Jesus with empty minds, when they neither refuse to raise any

215

questions about his life and work, nor ask too many questions, as if that also were a characteristic of the religious spirit, then it is not likely that such an honest and humble enterprise of endeavoring to understand the significance of Jesus Christ will leave inquirers with no more than empty words or send them away empty-handed.

INDEX

(a) Names and Subjects

Absolute, New Testament sense of the, 112, 200.
Act of God, the great, 195, 212.
Adam, Karl, 82.
Advent, the second, 56, 159.
Albertz, M., 28, 45.
Alternatives, false, 157.
Ambrose of Milan, 75, 146.
Amidah benediction, the, 178.
'Ancient of Days,' the, 184.
'Another Jesus'? 126f.
Anselm, 74, 185.
Anthony of Egypt, 62.
Antioch, the school of, 68f.
Anti-Semitism, 61.
'Apotheosis' theories of Jesus, 22f.
Aquinas, 66; his defective exegesis, 75, 78, 81, 82.
Arnold, Matthew, on the gospels, 24f.; on Jesus and St. Paul, 155.
Assimilating power of Christian faith, 158, 172.
Assimilations in text of the New Testament, 143f.
Atonement, day of, 196.
Augustine, and the gospels, 75, 142f., 149f.
Aurelius, Marcus, 103.
Authority of Jesus in his mission, 31, 37, 87, 90, 93f.
Autonomy of Jesus, 45.

Bach, 161.
Baptism of Jesus, 146.
Barabbas, 125.
Barnabas, epistle of, 120.
Baudissin, W. W. G., 177.
Beginning and the End, the, 181.
Belittling of Jesus in gospel criticism, 23, 26, 29f., 73.

Bezae, Codex, 119, 149.
Blake, 165.
Boullaye, H. Pinard de la, 117.
Brébeuf, Georges de, 66f.
Brooke, Stopford, 68.
Brunner, Emil, on Scripture and living faith, 210.
Bulgakov, S., on the Lord's real humanity, 82.
Bultmann, R., 27, 43, 81.
Burgon, Dean, 125.
Burkitt, F. C., 125, 145.
Burns, 67.
Bury, J. B., on history for its own sake, 51.

Caird, Edward, 53.
Cajetan, Cardinal, 83.
Calvin on the Lord's true humanity, 76, 82.
Campbell, McLeod, on prayer and the New Testament, 84.
Canon of the New Testament, its significance, 137, 163f.
Centre and circumference in Christianity, 20f., 162, 198f.
Change and the unchanging Christ, 160, 166f., 187, 199, 201, 206.
Chekhov, 205.
Christ, cosmic function of, 122; use of term in the New Testament, 129f.
Christianity, distinctiveness of, 31f., 51, 62, 152, 200; without Christ, 67; genesis of, 33, 154.
'Christians,' 129.
'Christ-like,' 105.
Church, memories of Jesus in the primitive, 33f., 40; responsibilities of the, 13f., 59, 64, 94f., 97, 212f.

219

INDEX

Luke's Gospel, 79, 80, 119f., 146-147.
Luther, 60, 108, 112.

Macarius Magnes, 139, 142, 148.
Mackail, J. W., 191.
Magi, the, 213f.
Magnificat, the, 59.
Marcion, 98, 140.
Mark's Gospel, 119, 132, 146.
Matthew's Gospel, 143-146.
Mendelssohn, Moses, 178.
Messianism and Jesus, 37, 126, 129f., 159.
Misgivings about Jesus, 190f., 213.
Montefiore, C. G., 134.
Moore, George, 127.
Moralizing of ancient historians, 49f.
Mozley, J. B., 64.
Myers, F. W. H., 193.

Neo-platonism, 139, 142.
New Testament, its gradual formation, 16f.; three religious implications in the, 200.
Nicene Creed, and Canon, 137; its terminology on the person of Christ, 61, 69f.
Nicholas of Cusa, 186.

'Once for all' in the New Testament, 57, 195.
Oral tradition, 27f.
Origen on the text of the gospels, 140, 145.

Past, religious interests in the, 114.
Paul, St., his knowledge of Jesus, 106, 155; his categories for Jesus, 152f.; his passion for, 136f.
Pedersen, J., 184.
'Pelican,' Jesus as the, 66.
Perspective in art, 20; in criticism of Jesus, 10f., 18f., 115, 163.
Peter, St., 23, 33, 119, 205.
Philo on the eternal God, 175-177.
'Piety' in Roman religion, 191.
Pilate, Pontius, 23, 64.

Plato on Socrates, 41f.
Polybius, 49.
Polycarp of Smyrna, 101.
Prayer-life of Jesus, 78-85.
Preaching Jesus, 60f.
Pringle-Pattison, Professor, 115.
Prophet, Jesus more than a, 38, 90.
Psalms, book of, in primitive Christianity, 81f.

Rabbi, Jesus as, 123f.
Raphael, 9.
Rashdall, Hastings, 91.
Realisation of Jesus, conditions for, 58, 113, 207f., 215.
Recognizing Jesus, 56.
Reitzenstein, R., 36.
Renan, 178.
Resurrection faith, origin of the, 33, 46.
Revelation, Scripture organic to, 209; the book of, 94, 183, 202.
Rich young ruler, story of the, 143f.
Rock of Ages, 173.
Rogers, Samuel, 211.
Rose, Professor H. J., on core of facts in the gospels, 46f.
Rossetti, C. G., 57.
Rothe, Richard, on the function of the Bible, 209.

Sabatier, Paul, 44.
Sacramental function of the Word, 172, 209.
Sacrifice of Jesus Christ, the, 88.
Sainte-Beuve, 111.
'Same,' twofold sense in which the Lord Jesus is the, 11f., 171f., 198.
Sellers, R. V., 68.
Seneca, 103.
Serapion of Antioch, 17.
Servant of the Lord, the, 183.
Shekinah, the, 89.
Sin, Christian sense of, 195f.; forgiveness of, 97.
Socrates, ancient interest in, 41f., 52.
Söderblom, N., 214.

220

(b) Texts

THE AUTHOR

JAMES MOFFATT holds degrees from Glasgow University and from St. Andrew's University in Scotland, the land of his birth. He has degrees also from Oxford University, in England; and from Dickinson College, in Carlisle, Pennsylvania. The years have brought him indisputable distinction as minister of the United Free Church of Scotland (1896-1912); Yates Professor of Greek in Mansfield College, Oxford (1912-15); Professor of Church History in Glasgow (1915-1927); Professor of Church History in Union Theological Seminary, New York City.

Dr. Moffatt is internationally known for his modern translation of the Bible and as the author of numerous religious books. Among the latter are *THE FIRST FIVE CENTURIES OF THE CHURCH* (one of the volumes of THE LONDON THEOLOGICAL LIBRARY), and the present volume—*JESUS CHRIST THE SAME*.

INDEX